CW00344340

Written by Rob Mason

A TWOCAN PUBLICATION

©2018. Published by twocan
under licence from West Ham United.

ISBN: 978-1-912692-50-7

PICTURE CREDITS:
Getty Images, Action Images,
Press Association.

A-Z
& 1-ELEVEN
OF WEST HAM
UNITED
ESSENTIAL
HAMMERS

A-Z & 1-Eleven

West Ham United are one of football's most revered institutions. They are the club of Bobby Moore, Geoff Hurst and Martin Peters – England's World Cup winning heroes of 1966. They are also the club of Trevor Brooking, a footballing personality who embodies all that is good within the game.

The Hammers are renowned not just for the trophies they have won but the manner in which they have won them. West Ham's style is to play with flair, to entertain and to attack.

Backed by some of the most vocal supporters in the game, a club that is the pride of East London is built on foundations set by the fact that in its first 89 years it only had five managers. They were men who helped make the club what it is today and of course they are all featured here, along with modern day managers, players and personalities.

This A-Z & 1-Eleven of the Hammers tries to bring to life many of the stories that illustrate just how fascinating a club West Ham United really are. The book is not a guide to every famous player, manager, game or incident the club have ever had. Instead it is a quirky collection of facts and stories to entertain fans, be they experts or beginners.

I first saw West Ham play in the early 1970s and I've had the pleasure of meeting Bobby Moore and many other club legends including Pop Robson and Paolo Di Canio. I hope you enjoy it and as well as having a few memories prompted, find out some stories you did not know about a club of such hidden depths.

Rob Mason

TREVOR BROOKING

Academy of Football

Virtually every club has an Academy for the development of young players but at West Ham United, 'The Academy of Football' has become a motto.

The Hammers are renowned for being proud of the club's style of play, the 'West Ham way.' This is personified by players of the class and style of Trevor Brooking, Alan Devonshire, Manuel Lanzini and of course the boys of '66. The fact that many of these stars have come through the club's youth system further emphasises that at West Ham it is not just about winning but how you win.

Antonio

From Tooting & Mitcham United to West Ham United and England squad selection, Michail Antonio's rise and rise shows how far a player can go when he works hard to maximise his talent.

The versatile Londoner made his name with Sheffield Wednesday after a series of loans from Reading. Moving to Nottingham Forest his upward trajectory continued leading the Hammers to bring him to the club where he became Hammer of the Year in 2016/17 and earned England call-ups.

JULIAN DICKS 1992/93

Anglo-Italian Cup

Cremonese, AC Reggiana, Cozena and Pisa were all met when West Ham competed in the Anglo-Italian Cup in 1992/93.

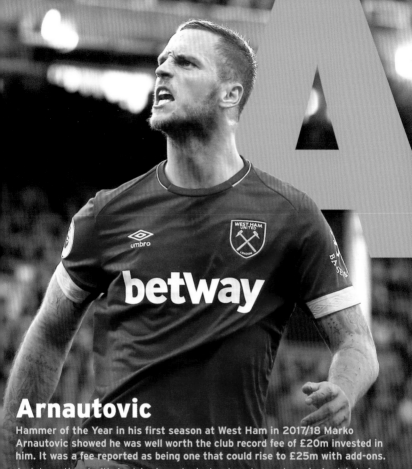

Arnautovic

Hammer of the Year in his first season at West Ham in 2017/18 Marko Arnautovic showed he was well worth the club record fee of £20m invested in him. It was a fee reported as being one that could rise to £25m with add-ons.

An international with Austria, Arnautovic developed as a player in Austria before coming to prominence in the Netherlands with Twente and from there he went on loan to Inter Milan. Next stop was a three-year spell in Germany with Werder Bremen before coming into English football with Stoke City for whom he played 125 Premier League games.

Arnautovic is the sort of player fans love to watch. An exciting player with brilliant control and a vicious shot, Marko is a player fans want to see given the ball whenever possible.

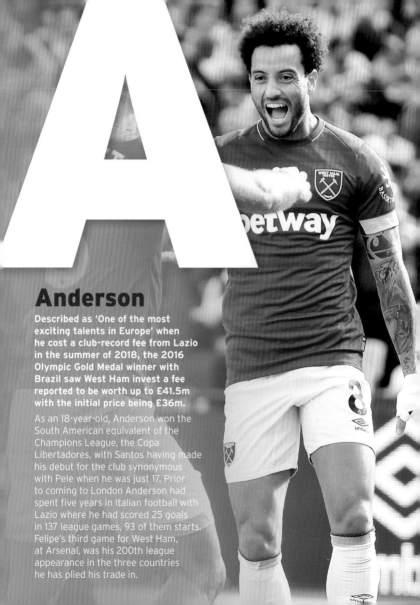

A

Anderson

Described as 'One of the most exciting talents in Europe' when he cost a club-record fee from Lazio in the summer of 2018, the 2016 Olympic Gold Medal winner with Brazil saw West Ham invest a fee reported to be worth up to £41.5m with the initial price being £36m.

As an 18-year-old, Anderson won the South American equivalent of the Champions League, the Copa Libertadores, with Santos having made his debut for the club synonymous with Pele when he was just 17. Prior to coming to London Anderson had spent five years in Italian football with Lazio where he had scored 25 goals in 137 league games, 93 of them starts. Felipe's third game for West Ham, at Arsenal, was his 200th league appearance in the three countries he has plied his trade in.

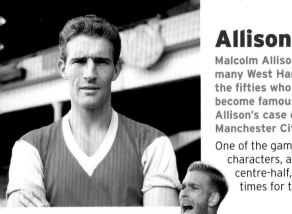

Allison

Malcolm Allison was one of many West Ham players from the fifties who went on to become famous managers, in Allison's case especially with Manchester City as 'Big Mal'.

One of the game's colourful characters, as a tactically astute centre-half, Allison played 255 times for the Irons.

Adrian

Goalkeeper Adrian has given the club good service since signing from Real Betis in his home country of Spain in June 2013. During his final campaign in Spain a highlight for Adrian was keeping a La Liga clean sheet in a 1-0 win over Real Madrid in November 2012 and he has risen to the big occasion more than once since joining the Irons.

His first four appearances came in the Capital One Cup prior to a Premier League debut away to Manchester United followed by a home league bow against Arsenal. In 2017/18 he kept seven clean sheets in 22 games including shut-outs against Chelsea, Arsenal and Manchester United.

Ashton

Winger Herbert Ashton scored 24 goals in 249 games for West Ham after joining in 1908.

A crowd puller who became something of an early cult hero, he asked ex-Hammer Danny Shea to be his Best Man when he married a local girl.

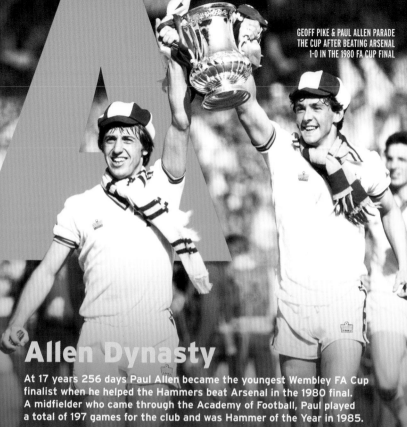

Allen Dynasty

At 17 years 256 days Paul Allen became the youngest Wembley FA Cup finalist when he helped the Hammers beat Arsenal in the 1980 final. A midfielder who came through the Academy of Football, Paul played a total of 197 games for the club and was Hammer of the Year in 1985.

Paul's cousin Clive also played for West Ham between 1992 and 1994. An England international, Clive was a goal machine who averaged marginally under a goal every two games for the Hammers and ended his well-travelled career with 197 goals from 407 league games.

The Allen family are a footballing dynasty which started with Les Allen signing for Chelsea in 1954. Les' brother Dennis topped 300 league games starting with Charlton. Clive Allen is the son of Les as is Bradley Allen who also played for Charlton during his career.

'Mad Dog' Martin Allen signed for West Ham in 1989 and is the cousin of Les and Bradley. Martin's son Charlie had a spell at Dagenham & Redbridge making seven Allens who have played senior football, three of them at West Ham.

Ashton

A brilliant centre-forward, Dean Ashton arrived from Norwich in 2006 and cost a club-record £7m.

Unfortunately, his career ended following injury after making his England debut.

HAMMER

OFFICIAL PROGRAMME · TENPENCE

ANGLO-ITALIAN
CUP WINNERS CUP
1975-76
Final
Second Leg

Boleyn Ground
Upton Park, London
WEDNESDAY
10 DECEMBER 1975
7.30 p.m.

WEST HAM UNITED

A.C. FIORENTINA (ITALY)

Anglo Italian Cup Winners' Cup

Fiorentina were faced in this short-lived competition in 1975/76, the Viola winning both legs 1-0.

Abandoned Matches

The lights went out at the Boleyn Ground in November 1997 during a match with Crystal Palace with the score at 2-2.

The first game abandoned at the stadium was also in November, 1948, as West Ham trailed 1-2 to Grimsby. In March 1952 a game was abandoned at half-time with the score 1-1 with Brentford. Two years later there were only seven minutes left when a 4-1 lead over Stoke was ruled to count for nothing and two days after Christmas in 1965 only half an hour of a goalless game with Aston Villa was played.

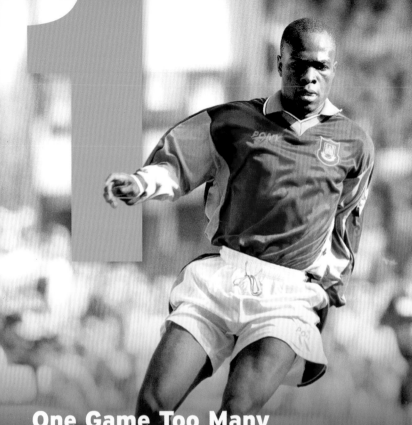

One Game Too Many

Manny Omoyinmi's one appearance in 1999/2000 lasted just seven minutes during which he apparently touched the ball twice during extra-time of a League Cup quarter-final with Aston Villa. His minimal contribution to the game would have been one of the tiniest footnotes in the club's entire history but for one thing. He was cup-tied.

Omoyinmi had played in the competition earlier in the season on loan to Gillingham but the player had forgotten and administratively no-one picked up on it. Subsequently Harry Redknapp's side had to replay the tie with Villa despite thinking that they had already made it into the semi-finals. Villa won the replay 3-1!

LUDEK MIKLOSKO

Goalkeepers

Traditionally number one is the goalkeeper's shirt.

West Ham have been so strong in the goalkeeping department down the years with great names such as Phil Parkes, Ludek Miklosko, Mervyn Day, Ernie Gregory, Ted Hufton and more recently Adrian and Lukasz Fabianski giving the Irons a solid base between the sticks.

Greatest Gate

West Ham United have always had a fantastic following, backed up by 2017/18's 56,885 average attendance.

West Ham United and Bolton Wanderers met in the first-ever Wembley FA Cup final in 1923. The Official attendance was given as 126,047, but in fact, tens of thousands more than the official figure actually saw the game.

One-Nil

'1-0 to the Arsenal' is a chant fans of the North London club at one time loved to sing in the days when their game was all about defence.

In the 1980 FA Cup final, 1-0 against the Arsenal was sufficient to bring the cup to the Boleyn Ground after Trevor Brooking used his head to nod the winner.

Boleyn

From 1904 until 2016 West Ham played at the Boleyn Ground, albeit many people referred to the stadium as Upton Park.

An urban myth had it that Anne Boleyn had met Henry VIII at the original house on Green Street adjacent to the Boleyn Ground. The original 'Boleyn Castle' was built on land given to Richard Breame in 1544 and it is possible Anne Boleyn's brother stayed there.

Bubbles

Written by James Kendis, James Brockman and Nat Vincent who conjured up the lyrics and John Kellette who wrote the music, the 1918 song, "I'm Forever Blowing Bubbles' was adopted by Hammers fans in the 1920s thanks to Charlie Paynter.

The song has been recorded by many artists including Vera Lynn, Doris Day, Cockney Rejects and the 1975 West Ham cup final squad.

Bond

John Bond came to West Ham in 1950 and won promotion in 1958 and the FA Cup six years later, leaving in 1966 after 444 games.

He was affectionately nicknamed 'Muffin' after the children's character Muffin the Mule due to the power of his defensive clearances. Although he went on to manage seven clubs he never returned to the Boleyn Ground hot-seat. His son Kevin had an extensive playing career and also moved into management.

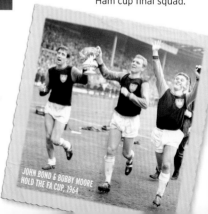

JOHN BOND & BOBBY MOORE HOLD THE FA CUP, 1964

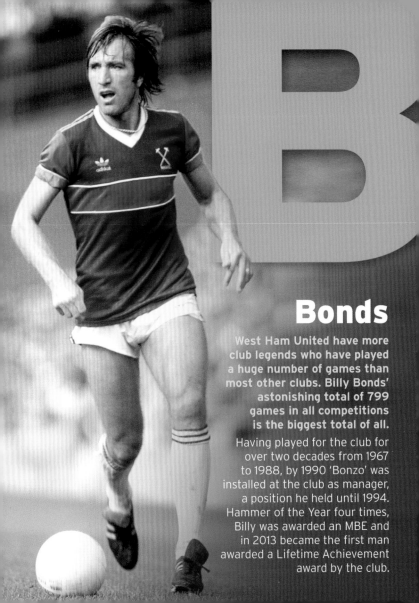

Bonds

West Ham United have more club legends who have played a huge number of games than most other clubs. Billy Bonds' astonishing total of 799 games in all competitions is the biggest total of all.

Having played for the club for over two decades from 1967 to 1988, by 1990 'Bonzo' was installed at the club as manager, a position he held until 1994. Hammer of the Year four times, Billy was awarded an MBE and in 2013 became the first man awarded a Lifetime Achievement award by the club.

Big

Big Mal and Big Sam had very different ways of playing the same game. Big Malcolm Allison was one of the class of the 1950s at West Ham to move into management. It was something the fedora-wearing, cigar-chomping Allison took to with flamboyance and no little success, winning a host of honours with Manchester City and Sporting Lisbon.

Big Sam in contrast had a well-travelled career as a player and even more well-travelled as a manager, a spell that included the briefest of stints in charge of England. Taking over a recently relegated West Ham in the summer of 2011, Allardyce secured immediate promotion via the Play-Offs and left the club in 2015 after back-to-back mid-table finishes back in the top flight.

Brooking

Sir Trevor Brooking is the living breathing embodiment of all that is good about West Ham United. As a footballer Brooking was brilliant, the kind of unhurried player who always had time on the ball.

Sublime in possession, Brooking's passing was world class. In all competitions he scored over 100 goals for the club but the least typical of his strikes was his most important, a close range header to win the 1980 FA Cup final. In addition to his 647 appearances for the club Sir Trevor had 14 more in two spells as caretaker – winning nine of them for a win percentage of over 64%!

Bilic

Croatia international defender Slaven Bilic played for and managed West Ham.

He managed just over double his 54 playing appearances as manager in 2015/17.

Budgie

Johnny Byrne was known as 'Budgie' as he was one of the game's great talkers.

He had plenty to talk about having scored eight goals in eleven games for England to go with his 79 goals in 156 league games for the Irons.

Bishop

Ian Bishop played over 100 more games for West Ham than any other of his ten clubs, turning out in over 250 league games for the Claret and Blues between 1989 and 1998.

With his often long hair and all-action style you could not miss the Bishop. The Hammers also had a Syd Bishop who played over 170 times in the 1920s.

Blackburn

Fred Blackburn was born in the town whose name he bore and perhaps inevitably started his career with the Rovers of that Lancastrian football town. Having won three caps for England Fred came to West Ham in 1905.

Known for his ball skills in an era when in bad weather the ball could be a dead weight, Blackburn played over 200 games for the Irons until 1913 and had a joint benefit game with George Kitchen, a goalkeeper who had earlier enjoyed a benefit match with Everton.

Brady

Karren Brady is one of the most recognisable and respected figures in football. Vice-Chairman of West Ham, she previously served as managing director at Birmingham City.

As a TV personality, newspaper columnist, novelist and Life Peer in the House of Lords, Baroness Brady is a hugely influential sporting executive and someone who has proved to be a major asset for the Irons.

Brady

Legendary Republic of Ireland schemer Liam Brady saved the best for last, completing a distinguished career with West Ham in the late eighties and 1990.

Having made his name with Arsenal Liam starred in Italy with Juventus, Sampdoria, Inter and Ascoli before coming back to London. He later managed Celtic and Brighton. Debuting for the Irons at home to Norwich in March 1987, Liam's first goal came the following month as he inspired his new team to a 3-1 victory at home to his old club Arsenal.

Brothers

Rio and Anton Ferdinand hail from Peckham and both developed as players through the West Ham Academy.

Anton played 138 league games during the first decade of the new millennium before a big-money move to Sunderland but the reported £8m fee paid for Anton was less than half the £18m Leeds had paid for his elder brother Rio in 2000. Eventually capped 81 times by England, Rio was Hammer of the Year when still a teenager and as a TV pundit is one of the most thoughtful and considered people on TV.

Boxing

There have many great nights at West Ham but not all of them have been about football! On 14 July 2012 over 30,000 came to the Boleyn Ground to see David Haye take on Dereck Chisora in a Heavyweight Boxing Contest.

Credit to Chisora who got back to his feet after twice being decked by 'the Hayemaker' in the opening five rounds. Haye enjoyed the night, noting, "This is the best atmosphere I've been in in my life."

Best

Clyde Best MBE was a pioneer for black players in the game. From 1968 to 1976 he was a powerful centre-forward who made many a goal for others through his physical prowess in addition to finding the net himself 47 times in 186 league appearances.

Born in Bermuda Best went on to play in the USA, the Netherlands and Canada after showing that the only colours that matter are the ones on your shirt and Clyde was quality in claret and blue.

Berkovic

In the late 1990s, the sight of Eyal Berkovic on the ball for the Irons was a sight to behold.

He was the man fans wanted on the ball. A midfield talent with a low centre of gravity Berkovic could make the ball talk, such was his control, while his range of passing was sublime.

Batman

Every club has celebrity supporters but how many can claim Batman?

Actor Christian Bale starred as the caped crusader in the Dark Knight trilogy and the Wales born Hollywood superstar has been seen at West Ham games.

Brand

Born when West Ham were FA Cup holders in 1975, comedian Russell Brand is a massive Hammers fan.

He even infamously planted a kiss on Irons manager Slaven Bilic in 2016 as he celebrated victory over Spurs.

Brown

Capped once by England and later the manager of Norwich, Shrewsbury and Plymouth, Ken Brown gave long service to West Ham, his first club, from 1953 to 1967.

A promotion winner who also won FA Cup and European Cup Winners' Cup medals, Brown had a Testimonial with the club before following his former teammate John Bond to Torquay and then ending his playing days at Hereford.

Billy

The best remembered contribution to the first ever Wembley final in 1923 was not one of the players or managers of either West Ham or Bolton Wanderers. Instead it was a white horse called Billy.

Seen on many a photograph, if not for Billy helping to get the crowd off the pitch the game would never have taken place. More people saw the game than any other match ever played in England. While the official attendance was 126,047 unofficial estimates claim more than twice that number attended Wembley's first final.

Right-Backs

Modern day squad numbers no longer automatically equate to positions on the pitch but traditionally the number two shirt has been the domain of the right-back.

Ray Stewart, Steve Potts, Alf Chalkley and John Bond are amongst those to wear the number two shirt with distinction.

RAY STEWART

Spot On

Julian Dicks twice scored two penalties in a game for the Irons.

In March 1993 he blasted both goals in a 2-0 win over Tranmere. Two and a half years later Dicks did it again with two successful spot kicks in a 2-1 win over Tranmere's near neighbours Everton.

Do It Again

Once is never enough if you enjoy something so it should come as no surprise that West Ham have twice achieved numerous honours.

The club were Division two champions in 1958 and 1981. When it comes to winning the Play-Offs the Irons did so in 2005 and 2012.
They have also played in two European Cup Winners' Cup finals, in 1965 and 1976 and two League Cup finals, 1966 and 1981.

MARK NOBLE & CHRIS POWELL
CHAMPIONSHIP PLAY-OFF FINAL 2005

It Takes Two

Famously Alan Taylor scored both goals in the final when West Ham won the FA Cup in 1975 but the former Rochdale striker seemed to have a thing about braces in that season's cup games.

He had also scored twice in the 2-1 semi-final win over Ipswich (after a goalless draw) and just for good measure in the quarter-final at Highbury he netted twice as Arsenal were beaten 2-0, meaning that in the four cup games he played that season he scored the club's last six goals of the cup run as the trophy was raised. Although Taylor played in 14 league games during that same season, guess how many goals he scored during those appearances? Two of course.

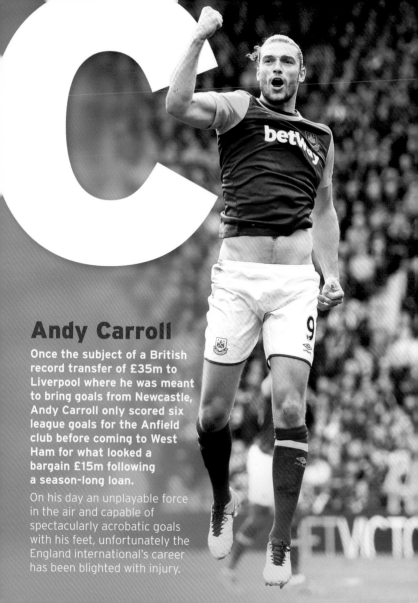

Andy Carroll

Once the subject of a British record transfer of £35m to Liverpool where he was meant to bring goals from Newcastle, Andy Carroll only scored six league goals for the Anfield club before coming to West Ham for what looked a bargain £15m following a season-long loan.

On his day an unplayable force in the air and capable of spectacularly acrobatic goals with his feet, unfortunately the England international's career has been blighted with injury.

Chicken Run

On the east side of the Boleyn Ground a former stand surrounded by the sort of wire you see on chicken coops resulted in the stand being nicknamed the Chicken run.

It was where some of West Ham's noisiest supporters used to be situated. The stand was demolished in 1969 to be replaced by the compact East Stand which carried on the nickname of the original chicken run.

Cup Winners' Cup

The European Cup Winners' Cup ran from 1960 to 1999. West Ham competed in it four times, winning it in 1965, being finalists in 1976, semi-finalists in 1966 and reaching the third round in 1981.

TSV Munich were beaten in the final at Wembley while just over a decade later it was West Ham's turn to play a final in the opponents city, going down to Anderlecht at the ill-fated Heysel Stadium in Brussels.

BOBBY MOORE

Claret & Blue

The kit known as the traditional West Ham kit, featuring light blue sleeves with a claret top, accompanied by white shorts and claret socks, was first seen in 1903.

While there have been variations, particularly with the socks which have frequently been white, and since the mid-1980s the sleeves have often been mainly claret, essentially the West Ham kit has succeeded in retaining its traditional feel.

Caretakers

Trevor Brooking served two spells as caretaker manager with the Hammers while Kevin Keen was called on even more often! Brooking stepped into the breach twice in 2003 while Keen acted as caretaker in 2006, 2008 and again in 2011 having twice been a promotion winner with the Hammers.

Previously Kevin had had a spell as caretaker boss with Macclesfield and would later manage Colchester. As a player, 219 of Keen's 502 league appearances had been with West Ham, more than with any of his quartet of other clubs.

KEVIN KEEN

Curbishley

Alan Curbishley started his career at West Ham as a midfielder in the second half of the seventies and returned to the club for his second managerial post over a quarter of a century later, rescuing the club from relegation and improving into a mid-table place during his one full season in control.

In between his spells at the Boleyn Ground 'Curbs' played for Birmingham, Aston Villa, Brighton and Charlton where he had two spells before managing the Addicks from 1991 to 2006.

Cottee

Goal-machine Tony Cottee enjoyed two successful spells with West Ham in the 1980s and 90s, sandwiching a stint at Everton.

He also won England honours and played in cup finals for Everton, Leicester and in Malaysia with Selangor.

AUGUST 1958 (L-R):
ERNIE GREGORY, JOHN BOND,
MALCOLM PYKE, ANDY NELSON,
VIC KEEBLE, NOEL CANTWELL,
JOHN DICK, KEN BROWN,
BILL LANSDOWNE, ANDY MALCOLM,
MIKE GRICE, MALCOLM MUSGROVE,
JOHN SMITH & BILL DARE.

Cantwell

Having the middle names
Euchuria Cornelius was not
the only notable thing about
Noel Cantwell. A stalwart of West
Ham during the 1950s, like many
of that era full-back Noel became
a manager having lengthy spells in
charge of Coventry City and Peterborough
United in addition to managing in the USA.

Capped 36 times by the Republic of Ireland the
versatile Cantwell also played up front, scoring more for
Ireland than he did in 248 league games at West Ham.

Cardiff

Cardiff's Millennium Stadium hosted West Ham three years in a row while it was being used for the biggest domestic games while Wembley was being rebuilt. From 2004 to 2006 the Hammers were annual visitors in the principality.

CHAMPIONSHIP PLAY-OFF
FINAL, 2004/05

Following the disappointment of losing the 2004 Play-Off final 1-0 to Crystal Palace, twelve months later it was a day of joy as Bobby Zamora's goal secured promotion as Preston North End were beaten in the Play-Off final as they had been in the 1964 FA Cup final. A further season on, it was the FA Cup final West Ham returned to Cardiff for. As the game ticked into injury-time there were high hopes that the Irons would win 3-2 as they had in 1964, only for Liverpool to equalise and go on to take the trophy on penalties.

Charity Shield

West Ham jointly won the Community Shield (formerly Charity Shield) in 1964 when they drew 2-2 with League Champions Liverpool at Anfield. Johnny Byrne and Geoff Hurst scored equalisers for the cup-holding Hammers to level goals from Gordon Wallace and Gerry Byrne.

West Ham also took part in the pre-season show-piece in 1975 losing 2-0 to champions Derby in the second such game to be staged at Wembley. Five years later West Ham again played for the Shield at Wembley, once again facing Liverpool who this time won with a Terry McDermott goal.

Cross

Well-travelled centre-forward David Cross scored a hat-trick in that game against Castilla.

In five years at the Boleyn Ground from 1977 to '82 he also bagged 78 league goals for the club, winning the FA Cup and promotion along the way.

Closed Doors

Only 262 people (all staff and media) came to see Real Madrid play in European competition at West Ham.

That's not strictly true but when Real's reserve side Real Madrid Castilla qualified for Europe and played at the Boleyn Ground the game was ordered to be played behind closed doors following crowd trouble in the first leg. West Ham won 5-1.

Dick

John Dick scored almost a goal for every two of the 377 games he played for the club from the early fifties to the early sixties, netting 177 times.

Capped once by Scotland, it was during Dick's time at West Ham that he appeared against England at Wembley in 1959. The cap made him the first Hammer to be capped by the Scots.

Dicks

Defender Julian Dicks became a cult hero in his 326 games for the club during which he was Hammer of the Year in 1990, 1992, 1996 and 1997 having been runner-up in 1989.

The possessor of a fearsome shot, he fired home 65 goals for the club, 34 of them penalties. Bristol born, Julian began with Birmingham and played for Liverpool in between two spells with the Hammers. He was capped at B and Under 21 level by England.

Defoe

Beckton-born Jermain Defoe played youth football for Charlton before debuting for West Ham. Defoe made his name in a record-breaking loan to Bournemouth where he netted in a league record eleven successive games and who he would sign for as a veteran in 2017.

Jermain left West Ham in 2004 in a deal that brought Bobby Zamora and £6.7m from Tottenham Hotspur. For England Defoe scored 20 times in 57 appearances, only 22 of which were starts.

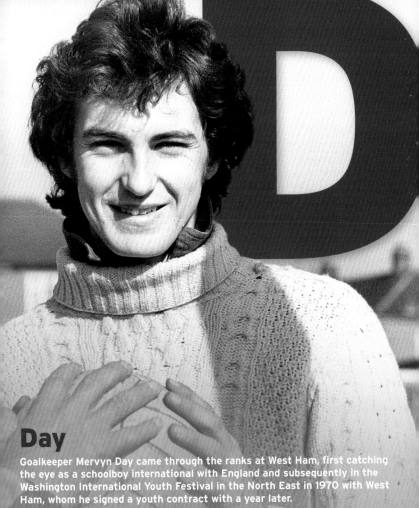

Day

Goalkeeper Mervyn Day came through the ranks at West Ham, first catching the eye as a schoolboy international with England and subsequently in the Washington International Youth Festival in the North East in 1970 with West Ham, whom he signed a youth contract with a year later.

A first-team debut came in August 1973, becoming the youngest FA Cup final goalkeeper two years later when he kept a clean sheet and became PFA Young Player of the Year. He also played in the 1976 European Cup Winners' Cup final and later played extensively for Leeds and managed Carlisle where he finished his goalkeeping career.

Di Canio

Without doubt Di Canio played the best football of his career at West Ham. He also played more games for the Hammers than any of his other ten clubs. He was a maverick who was given a chance at the Boleyn Ground by Harry Redknapp after being given a lengthy suspension for pushing a referee over when he was with Sheffield Wednesday.

Paolo repaid the club many times over with a mixture of magic, madness and magnanimity. The man who came to the club with the cloud of having floored a referee was to win the FIFA Fair Play award after catching the ball rather than scoring against Everton when their 'keeper Paul Gerrard was stricken. Di Canio liked his goals to have a touch of class - none more so than the scissor-kick volley against Wimbledon that was the BBC's Goal of the Season and Sky's Goal of the Decade.

Dickens

Plaistow-born Alan Dickens played over 200 games for the Hammers during the 1980s having won the FA Youth Cup at the start of the decade.

A debut goal against Notts County in 1982 was the stuff of dreams for the midfielder who gained England Under 21 honours. After his playing days he became a black cab driver.

Devonshire

Hammer of the year in 1979 having been runner-up two years earlier, Alan Devonshire was a midfield schemer who seemed to float over the grass.

Elegant and lithe, Devonshire in possession was a glorious sight and he was named in the PFA Division Two team of the year in consecutive seasons in the late seventies and early eighties. Capped eight times by England, Alan's father Leslie Devonshire had played for Crystal Palace in the early fifties.

Drake

Ted Drake scored more than a goal a game for England and 171 goals in 238 league games for Southampton and Arsenal before World War Two but did you know he played twice for West Ham during the war?

He also managed Reading and Chelsea and played cricket for Hampshire.

ALAN SEALEY, EUROPEAN CUP WINNERS' CUP FINAL, 1965

Entertainers

"This was our greatest game... a tremendous advertisement for football" remarked Ron Greenwood after the Hammers had become princes of Europe when lifting the European Cup Winners' Cup at Wembley in 1965.

Playing entertaining and attractive football is what West Ham United is all about. Winning is welcome but how West Ham win is most important and that is one of the things that sets the Irons apart from many a club.

Extra-Time

Extra-time is always something that makes special demands on players. The Hammers played extra-time in the 2006 FA Cup final against Liverpool, drawing 3-3 before losing on penalties.

Ten years later Liverpool were beaten with a goal in injury-time of extra-time as Angelo Ogbonna headed the winner as the Reds were defeated 2-1.

ANGELO OGBONNA

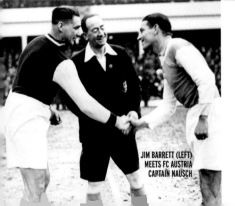
JIM BARRETT (LEFT) MEETS FC AUSTRIA CAPTAIN NAUSCH

Ever-Presents

Percy Allen was the first player to go through an entire season playing in every league game. He appeared in all 42 games in 1921/22.

Later that decade Jim Barrett was ever present in consecutive campaigns while in the thirties Joe Cockroft managed to not miss a game for an incredible four seasons in a row. More recently Jussi Jaaskelainen achieved the feat in 2012/13.

European Cup Winners' Cup

West Ham played in two European Cup Winners' Cup finals, winning one and losing one. The 97,974 who saw West Ham beat 1860 Munich at Wembley in 1965 was the biggest attendance at such a final until Barcelona beat Standard Liege in front of 100,000 at the Camp Nou in Barcelona in 1982.

In 1976, West Ham played in the final in Brussels against Anderlecht, losing 4-2. The 1965 final was a great game in which Alan Sealey broke the deadlock in the 69th minute and wrapped things up two minutes later. In '76 the Hammers led in Belgium through Holland - Pat Holland - but eventually succumbed.

Fenton

Born in Forest Gate in 1914, Ted Fenton became West Ham's third-ever manager in 1950 having at one time been sent to bring beer for the first manager Syd King. Fenton played for West Ham, debuting in 1932/33 and scoring a hat-trick in his second season against Bury.

After World War Two Ted managed Colchester before becoming assistant at West Ham where he succeeded Charlie Paynter in 1950. Fenton is credited with establishing the club's famed youth policy. He also led the Irons to promotion in 1958, leaving the Boleyn Ground three years later and going on to manage Southend United.

Full English

West Ham's 1975 FA Cup winning team were the last all-English team to win the cup.

The line-up was: Mervyn Day, John McDowell, Frank Lampard (Senior), Billy Bonds, Tommy Taylor, Kevin Lock, Billy Jennings, Graham Paddon, Alan Taylor, Trevor Brooking, Pat Holland, sub: Bobby Gould. Alan Taylor scored both of the goals in the final against Fulham and just for good measure manager John Lyall was English too.

Foreman

George Foreman may have grilled a few opponents but the player by this name at West Ham was someone who mainly played during World War Two.

He had managed a handful of games in peace-time, scoring his only goal in a win over Millwall in March 1939. After the war he played 36 league games for Spurs.

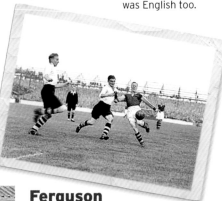

Ferguson

Scotland international goalkeeper Bobby Ferguson played a total of 276 games for the Hammers having cost a British-record fee for a goalkeeper of £65,000 when signed from Kilmarnock in 1967.

Having debuted in August of that year Ferguson's final game for the Irons came in November 1979 where he signed off at Chelsea. Perhaps inspired by a career as a 'keeper, Bobby is reported to have run a diving business after his playing days.

FA Amateur Cup Finals

West Ham staged no fewer than five finals of the FA's major competition, the FA Amateur Cup. All of these show-piece finals took place in the 1930s with Dulwich Hamlet winning the trophy three times at the Boleyn Ground.

They won the cup at West Ham in 1932, 1934 and 1937 defeating Marine 7-1 in 1932 and Leyton on the other occasions by 2-1 and 2-0. The first of the Boleyn Ground finals saw Illford defeat Bournemouth Gasworks Athletic 5-1 in 1930 while in 1936 Illford lost 2-0 to Casuals in a replay.

DULWICH HAMLET AMATEUR FOOTBALL TEAM AT UPTON PARK

Fabianski

Poland international 'keeper Lukasz Fabianski joined West Ham from Swansea City in the summer of 2018 after being their Player of the Year in his final season in Wales.

In four seasons with Swansea, he missed only three league games.

Fredericks

Ryan Fredericks arrived at the club on 1 July 2018 from Fulham on a free transfer.

Hammersmith born, the defender played over 100 times for Fulham after joining from Bristol City.

FRANK O'FARRELL IN ACTION IN AN
EARLY FLOODLIT HOME GAME, 1954

F

Floodlights

The first floodlit match at the Boleyn Ground was on Thursday 16 April 1953 against Spurs who were beaten 2-1. In 1955/56 and 1956/57 West Ham took part in a competition called the Southern Floodlit Cup winning it at the first time of asking after beating Aldershot 2-1 in the final after knocking out Crystal Palace at home and Reading away.

The following year Leyton Orient were beaten only for the Hammers to be eliminated by Arsenal in a replay after a 1-1 draw at the Boleyn Ground. The very first floodlit games involving the club came way back in the early days of Thames Ironworks in the 19th century when games at Hermit Road in Canning Town saw the ball whitewashed to make it easier to see as games were played under electric light! It is believed that West Bromwich Albion and Arsenal were the first teams to visit to try out the new system.

3

Hat-Trick Hurst

Hat-tricks are rare. Scoring one is always a notable achievement for any player, no matter how regular a goalscorer they are. When he was a West Ham United player Geoff Hurst scored the most famous and the most important hat-trick there has ever been in the history of football anywhere in the world. Hurst is the only man to ever hit a hat-trick in a World Cup final.

It is something that not even Pele, Maradona, Muller, Cruyff, Messi or either of the Ronaldos have ever been able to equal. In 1966 as England beat West Germany, Hurst had scored once in the first 90 minutes and added two more in extra-time.

FRANK LAMPARD SENIOR

Left-Backs

Frank Lampard senior, Jack Burkett, Julian Dicks and Noel Cantwell...

...are good examples of players who have excelled in the left-back position at West Ham throughout the decades, albeit shirt numbers did not exist in the game's early years before the number three became associated with the position.

Hat-trick of 'Keepers

Alvin Martin did not just score a hat-trick in the 8-1 win over Newcastle United in April 1986, he achieved the feat by scoring against three different goalkeepers.

Alvin's first was netted against Martin Thomas, the second came against Chris Hedworth and his hat-trick was converted past England forward Peter Beardsley.

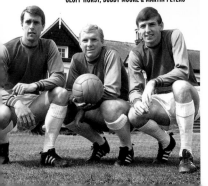

GEOFF HURST, BOBBY MOORE & MARTIN PETERS

Cup Final Hat-Trick

When West Ham's trio of Bobby Moore, Geoff Hurst and Martin Peters won the World Cup with England in 1966 they certainly were not fazed by being in a cup final.

West Ham had played in three cup finals in the three previous seasons. Most recently there had been the League Cup final, in March '66, lost on aggregate to West Brom after the Irons had won the first leg. The previous season the European Cup Winners' Cup had been won at Wembley with the same venue hosting the Hammers FA Cup victory of 1964.

Greenwood

Ron Greenwood is one of the greatest names in West Ham's rich history.
As a player Greenwood won the league title with Chelsea in 1955 and also
represented Bradford, Brentford and Fulham. Before coming to West Ham
Greenwood coached at Arsenal as well as with the England Youth and Under
23 teams. When he came to West Ham in 1961 Ron was the first West Ham
manager to have no previous links with the Hammers but he would become
synonymous with all that is good about one of the game's greatest clubs.

Greenwood assembled teams combining home-groomed players and astute signings.
In 1964 he led the team to the FA Cup and added the European Cup Winners' Cup
a year later. In 1974 Ron 'moved upstairs' to take over as General Manager at the
club leaving three years later to spend five years as England manager.

Gold

Born in 1936 in Stepney, David Gold is West Ham's Joint-Chairman.

Mr Gold was raised at 442 Green Street right next to the Boleyn Ground and has West Ham United in his blood and even played for the club as a schoolboy but was unable to accept an apprenticeship due to family commitments.

JIMMY COLLINS

Golden Hammer

Golden Hammer was the name of a greyhound which was runner up in the 1931 Greyhound Derby.

It was owned by Jimmy Collins who played 336 games for West Ham between 1923/24 and 1935/36. From 5 December 1925 until 20 April 1929 he never missed a game!

Grant

Avram Grant managed West Ham in 2010/11. As Israel manager, Grant's side had been unbeaten at the 2006 World Cup after which he led Chelsea to the Champions League final (where they lost to Manchester United on penalties) and also took Portsmouth to the FA Cup final in 2010.

Unfortunately, Grant could not bring success to East London and left after a single unsuccessful season.

Goddard

Paul Goddard played almost 100 more games for West Ham than any of his other five clubs. He was good value for the club record £800,000 he cost from his first club QPR in 1980.

A sharp, classy striker Goddard was a goal every three games man, scoring 71 times in 213 appearances. A scorer in the 1981 League Cup final, he was top scorer for the club two seasons later. In between those events Paul scored on his England debut but despite that goal was never given another opportunity.

Gale

Nicknamed 'Reggie' when he was at West Ham because his humour reminded his teammates of Reggie Kray, Tony Gale made 300 league appearances for the club having cost £200,000 from his first club Fulham.

A terrific defender and great character, as a veteran Gale went on to be part of Blackburn Rovers' Premier League winning squad in 1994/95.

Gregory

Goalkeeper Ernie Gregory gave long service to West Ham, his only club.

Having joined as a boy before World War Two he debuted after it and played 382 league games, being ever-present three times.

Greaves

West Ham were the final professional club of Jimmy Greaves, one of the finest natural finishers English football has ever been blessed with. A member of the English football Hall of Fame no one has scored more hat-tricks for England than Greaves' six.

Famously injury cost Greaves his place in England's 1966 World Cup team, where he was replaced by West Ham's World Cup final hat-trick hero Geoff Hurst who became his teammate at Upton Park. Ironically, when Greaves came to the club it was the Hammers' other World Cup final scorer Martin Peters he came in part exchange for. After his playing days he enjoyed great popularity as a TV presenter with former Liverpool and Scotland striker Ian St John.

Hurst

Only once every four years can anyone threaten Sir Geoff Hurst's unique record of being the only man to ever score a hat-trick in a World Cup final, a feat Hurst achieved for England in 1966 when he was on West Ham's books. Pele, Muller, Maradona and Messi are amongst those who have tried and failed but Hurst's hat-trick remains the only one.

Two years after Hurst's heroics at Wembley, he incredibly scored a double hat-trick for the Hammers - scoring six goals in one match as Sunderland's record defeat of 8-0 was equalled at the Boleyn Ground. Hurst was not simply a goal-poacher, he was a big strong forward who worked for the team and brought other people into play. His father Charlie had been a professional player. Geoff was not just a big-game specialist, he averaged a goal for every two of the near 500 games he played for the club before moving on to Stoke. He also played for WBA and in the USA with Seattle Sounders. As a manager he later took charge at Chelsea.

Hammers

The sign of two crossed rivet Hammers is famed throughout football.

West Ham's origins stem from when the club were known as Thames Ironworks, hence the fact the club are also known as the Irons.

Hooper

As with Frank Lampard you could not chant, 'There's only one Harry Hooper'...

The Hammers' winger's father of the same name had captained Sheffield United in the 1936 FA Cup final and came to West Ham as a trainer in 1950 - six years before the younger Hooper signed.

Hilsdon

George Hilsdon was a star of the club's early years.

An England international, he played for Boleyn Castle as a boy and starred for Chelsea between his spells at the Boleyn Ground, scoring five goals on his debut for them.

Hufton

Goalkeeper Ted Hufton played over 400 peace-time games for West Ham starting in the club's first-ever Football League game in 1919 until the final game of the 1931/32 campaign.

Prior to his league debut Hufton had played as a guest player for the club during the Great War after being wounded when serving with the Coldstream Guards. Before the war Ted had played for Sheffield United. Known for being a great penalty saver, Hufton was an England international and also played at Wembley in the first FA Cup final it staged, in 1923.

HEBDEN & HENDERSON

H

Hufton, Henderson, Hebden, Horlor and Hodgson put the H into Ham during the 1920s as West Ham often played with a five strong H-team.

Holland

Patsy Holland was not from the Netherlands. Indeed he was a Londoner from Poplar who starred for West Ham from just before the seventies until just after them.

He played almost 300 games including the FA Cup final in 1975 and the European Cup Winners' Cup final a year later when he scored.

Hat-tricks

Hat-trick heroes hog the headlines for good reason, scoring three goals in one match is an achievement to celebrate. Players such as Vic Watson, Syd Puddefoot and Danny Shea were serial hat-trick heroes.

Puddefoot got the Irons' first Football League hat-trick in 1920 against Port Vale while Fred Corbett had scored the first in the Southern League 19 years earlier against Wellingborough Town. Even earlier than that Billy Grassam bagged a FA Cup hat-trick against Clapton in 1900. The League Cup began in 1960 with Johnny Byrne claiming the club's first hat-trick in that competition two years later. David Cross notched the first hat-trick in European competition against Castilla in 1980.

Internationals

In modern times West Ham's squad is full of international footballers from around the world. William Jones became the first man capped while with the club when he was selected by Wales for games with England and Scotland in 1902.

The club's first England international was George Webb who was chosen for a game against Wales in 1911 – and he scored in a 3-0 win. It was 1959 when John Dick became the first man capped for Scotland while with West Ham and 14 years later Bertie Lutton completed the set when he became the first Iron to appear for Northern Ireland. There had been a Republic of Ireland international who was a Hammer before World War Two, Charlie Turner playing against Norway in 1937.

Irons

West Ham are nicknamed the Irons as well as the Hammers. The Irons comes from the club's early name of Thames Ironworks.

Scunthorpe United are known as the Iron, due to the town's history as a centre of Iron and Steelworks, but Scunthorpe are simply the Iron whereas at West Ham the call is 'Come On You Irons!'

Intertoto

West Ham 'won' the Intertoto Cup in 1999 – so did Juventus and Montpelier!

The Intertoto Cup was effectively an early season entry into a place in the UEFA Cup for the three winners. West Ham defeated Jokerit of Finland, Herenveen of the Netherlands and Metz of France in one of the three finals.

Ivory Coast v Italy

One of the internationals staged at the Boleyn Ground featured Ivory Coast against Italy.

The game in August 2010 saw the African country win 1-0 in a match when Mario Balotelli made his full debut for Italy. Kolo Toure got the only goal of the game with a header as he played alongside his brother Yaya.

Jennings

A fee of £110,000 made Billy Jennings one of John Lyall's first signings for the club.

The ex-Watford striker immediately began repaying what was a near club record fee at the time by getting a goal on his debut and helped the Irons to win the FA Cup during his first season.

Jones

William Jones was the first West Ham player to play for Wales but would give his life in the Great War.

A Private in the Royal Welch Fusiliers Jones was killed in action in Salonika in Greece on 6 May 1918. He had debuted for the Irons at home to Swindon in the Southern League eleven days before Christmas in 1901. He was on the winning side in two thirds of his 15 appearances for the club.

CROWD OF THE 1930S

James

Wilf James played for West Ham at the start of the 1930s, winning his two caps for Wales while with the club.

Both of his caps came in 1931 against Ireland, Wilf enjoying a 3-2 win at Wrexham on his debut but later being on the receiving end of a 4-0 defeat in Belfast. An inside left James scored seven times in 41 league and cup appearances having joined from Notts County but later moved on to Charlton Athletic.

Jarvis

Winger Matt Jarvis signed for West Ham in 2012 for an undisclosed fee that was recognised as a club record nonetheless.

Although his first season saw the England international provide the most crosses from open play in the league he scored only twice, a quarter of the number he had managed in his last full season with Wolves.

After a second season with an almost identical record in terms of games and goals the Teessider went on loan to Norwich City part of the way through his third season and in all competitions ended up playing 90 times for the Irons, scoring six times.

BILLY BONDS

Right-Half

The old right-half position was associated with the player wearing the number four shirt. In modern football the player assigned this shirt as a squad number still often operates in this midfield berth although sometimes central defenders wear it.

Jimmy Collins and Andy Malcolm are good examples of great right-halves to play for West Ham and while he could operate in numerous roles Billy Bonds played much of his best football in this position.

Four Goal Brown

Ken Brown scored just four goals in 455 games for the club between 1953 and 1967. Centre-half Ken did not score at all until his eleventh season when he netted in 5-0 and 3-1 home wins over Birmingham City and Manchester United in 1962/63.

On the final day of the 1964/65 season he scored in another home win, this time against Blackpool before finally scoring away from home, but in a defeat, at Northampton in October '65.

Four Seasons

Carlton Cole was West Ham's top scorer for four successive seasons from 2008/09 to 2011/12.

Tallies of ten, ten, eleven and 15 made Carlton a man for all seasons in a spell that climaxed with promotion via the Play-offs.

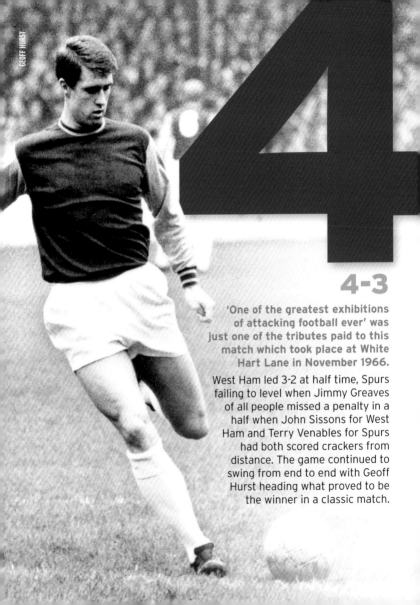

GEOFF HURST

4

4-3

'One of the greatest exhibitions of attacking football ever' was just one of the tributes paid to this match which took place at White Hart Lane in November 1966.

West Ham led 3-2 at half time, Spurs failing to level when Jimmy Greaves of all people missed a penalty in a half when John Sissons for West Ham and Terry Venables for Spurs had both scored crackers from distance. The game continued to swing from end to end with Geoff Hurst heading what proved to be the winner in a classic match.

King

One of the most important men in West Ham's history, Syd King was in charge of the club from 1902 for 30 years.

As a player he was reputed to have scored an infamous hat-trick of own goals when with Northfleet and before taking over as secretary/manager he had spent three seasons playing for West Ham in the days when they were still called Thames Ironworks. It was under King that West Ham entered the Football League and it was under him that they reached the first ever Wembley cup final in 1923.

Keeble

Ted Fenton knew exactly what he was getting when he signed Vic Keeble from Newcastle in 1957. Fenton had previously managed Keeble at Vic's home town club of Colchester.

A goal machine, Keeble struck 49 times in 80 games over two and a half seasons before injury ruined his career which at the Boleyn Ground had thrived through his partnership with John Dick.

Kay

A star of the twenties, George Kay played over 250 games including the 1923 'white horse' final in which he captained the Irons.

He later managed Southampton for whom he signed Vic Watson from West Ham before taking over at Liverpool where he won the title.

Kirkup

Joe Kirkup represented Northumberland at rugby but went on to play football for England Under 23s and play 187 times for West Ham.

The pinnacle of his career being the winning of the European Cup Winners' Cup in 1965.

Kitchen

G. KITCHEN.

Many a defender can match George Kitchen's Irons record of scoring six goals in just over 200 appearances - the thing is Kitchen was a goalkeeper, a penalty-taking goalkeeper.

Kitchen was a talented and confident sportsman who was a professional golfer when he signed from Everton in 1905 and went back to being a golf pro after his football career. Derbyshire born, Kitchen worked at a golf club near Bournemouth having ended his goalkeeping career with Southampton.

Kinsell

Already reaching veteran stage when Ted Fenton brought him to the Boleyn Ground, fifties full-back Harry Kinsell played over 100 games spread over five seasons as a dependable and experienced high-class footballer.

He had represented England in 'Victory' internationals.

Keane

The Republic of Ireland's all-time record and also youngest scorer, Robbie Keane had a four month cameo with West Ham on loan from Spurs in 2011 before joining LA Galaxy.

Signed by Avram Grant, Keane marked his Irons debut with a goal in an away win at Blackpool and added another goal against Aston Villa who he would join on loan from LA Galaxy the following year.

Konchesky

Barking-born Paul Konchesky cost West Ham £1.5m from Charlton in 2005. The club made a tidy profit when selling him to Fulham for more than twice that two years later and the Cottagers were also quids-in when selling him on to Liverpool for a further profit.

Konchesky already had a reason to be fond of the Boleyn Ground before he joined the Irons. As a Charlton player he had made his full England debut at West Ham against Australia in 2003. He would also be capped while with West Ham, coming on as a half-time sub for Wayne Bridge in a 3-2 win over Argentina in a match played in Geneva in November 2005.

Lyall

One of the greatest figures in the history of West Ham United, John Lyall served the club from 1955 to 1989, going from office boy to manager. Ilford born, Lyall represented England at West Ham at youth level and made his first team debut for the club in 1960. Sadly, injury ended his playing days just three years later but he carved out another career in coaching. After working successfully alongside Ron Greenwood Lyall became team manager in 1974 and assumed full control three years later when Greenwood answered England's call.

Under Lyall, the Irons twice won the FA Cup, in 1975 and 1980 as well as reaching the finals of the European Cup Winners' Cup in 1976 and the League Cup in 1981. In addition to an excellent cup record, Lyall led the club to its highest ever league position of third in 1986.

Lampard

The legendary Frank Lampard senior played over 650 games for West Ham from the mid-sixties to the mid-eighties, being ever present in the league in 1973/74.

He played in four cup finals under John Lyall's leadership. Capped twice by England, East Ham-born Frank is the father of Frank Lampard junior.

Lampard

Frank Junior won 106 caps for England and played the bulk of his career with Chelsea where he became that club's all-time leading scorer – an amazing achievement for a midfielder.

The younger Lampard commenced his career at the Boleyn Ground while his dad was on the coaching staff. After going on loan to Swansea Frank debuted for West Ham against Coventry in 1996, the first of 187 appearances for the club. In 2018 he began his managerial career with Derby County.

London Stadium

The London Stadium has been West Ham's huge home since August 2016. The Irons are now able to accommodate regular attendances of over 50,000 in a venue originally built for the 2012 Olympics.

Famed the world over for those games, its renown is growing season by season as a top Premier League arena.

Macari

No West Ham manager had been in charge for less than a decade at the time Lou Macari was appointed in 1989 but the following year the Scots-born son of Italian parents was dismissed.

Macari had actually spent six years of his childhood living at Forest Gate near Upton Park. He made his name as a sharp striker at Celtic and starred for Manchester United and Scotland before becoming manager of Swindon. Following his spell at West Ham, Macari went on to manage Birmingham, Stoke, Celtic and Huddersfield.

McDowell

John McDowell came through the ranks at 'the Academy of Football' which is West Ham.

Throughout the 1970s he was a stalwart in defence, being part of the FA Cup winning team in 1975. In total McDowell played just under 300 times for the club.

McGiven

Mick McGiven played during the successful cup run of his first club Sunderland in 1973. He had the almost impossible task of trying to succeed Bobby Moore, who he played alongside five times.

Unfortunately, injury brought McGiven's career to a premature end, after which he coached at the club before linking up with John Lyall at Ipswich and later working for Chelsea.

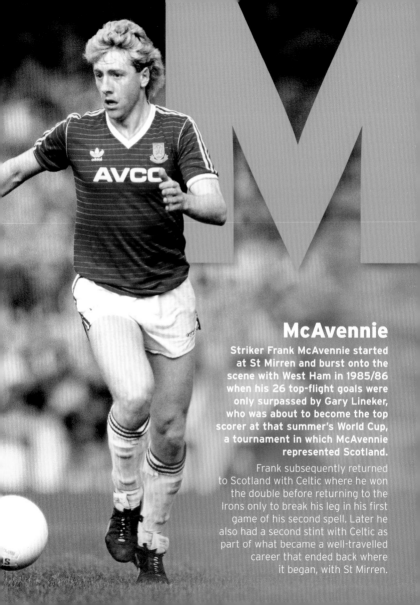

McAvennie

Striker Frank McAvennie started at St Mirren and burst onto the scene with West Ham in 1985/86 when his 26 top-flight goals were only surpassed by Gary Lineker, who was about to become the top scorer at that summer's World Cup, a tournament in which McAvennie represented Scotland.

Frank subsequently returned to Scotland with Celtic where he won the double before returning to the Irons only to break his leg in his first game of his second spell. Later he also had a second stint with Celtic as part of what became a well-travelled career that ended back where it began, with St Mirren.

Moore

Bobby Moore completed an incredible hat-trick by captaining teams to domestic, European and World trophies in consecutive years. With West Ham Bobby followed up the 1964 FA Cup with the European Cup Winners' Cup a year later, topped off by skippering England to the World Cup in 1966.

Footballer of the year in '64, 'Mooro' was the legends' legend. In addition to 644 appearances for the Irons, no-one could match his 108 caps for England when he retired and no-one can yet match his achievement of holding aloft the World Cup for the Three Lions.

Bobby Moore was the epitome of the composed footballer. Top modern day teams like to play the ball out from the back, there was no-one better at this than Bobby. Unhurried, calm, strong and supremely talented, the iconic image of him dispossessing Pele at the 1970 World Cup is another indelible memory of how the West Ham captain was the best defender in the world.

Moore

Bobby was not the only Moore to be a West Ham great. In the 1920s Billy Moore played just over 200 times, scoring almost exactly a goal for every four games.

His goals to games average was markedly better for England but despite scoring twice on his debut for the national side he was never picked again.

NORMAN CORBETT HAVING A KNEE MASSAGE FROM TRAINER BILLY MOORE

Messi

Lionel Messi may not be as good as the best ever player to play at the Boleyn Ground (that would be Bobby Moore!) but he came close.

Magical Messi played at West Ham for Argentina against Croatia on 12 October 2014 – scoring the winning goal from the penalty spot as Croatia were defeated 2-1.

Martin

In 20 years as a West Ham centre-back where he reached almost 600 appearances, Merseysider Alvin Martin gave tremendous service to West Ham.

He emerged from the club's prestigious youth system which his sons David and Joe were later members of. Alvin was capped 17 times by England.

Moyes

David Moyes won nine, drew ten and lost twelve of his games in charge of West Ham from November 2017 to May 2018. Before joining the Hammers he had had short spells with Sunderland, Real Sociedad and Manchester United.

Previously he had spent eleven years in charge of Everton and four with Preston where he ended his playing days. Preston won promotion under his guidance while Manchester United won the Community Shield under his management.

Miklosko

Czech international goalkeeper Ludek Miklosko became a real hero in over 300 games for the Irons for whom he later became goalkeeping coach.

Signed by Lou Macari in 1990, Miklosko had the unenviable task of taking over from Phil Parkes but proved to be a huge success until his sale to QPR in 1998.

Memorial Grounds

The Memorial Grounds was the club's home immediately before moving to the Boleyn Ground.

Seven years were spent at the Memorial Grounds, the pitch was surrounded by a cycling track while there were also tennis courts. Brentford were beaten 1-0 in the first match there on 11 September 1897.

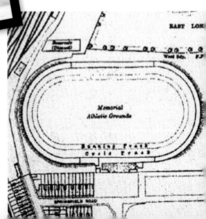

Moustaches

Modern day supporters may take part in 'Mo-vember' but a trawl through the photographic archives reveals that the Hammers have had some spectacular moustaches through the ages!

Syd King, who managed the club for the first three decades of the twentieth century sported a wonderful 'tache as did Billy Grassam who scored four goals on his debut at the start of the last century. Club founder Arnold Hills had a moustache that must have got in the way of his soup but perhaps the best of them all was sported by Syd King's successor Charlie Paynter!

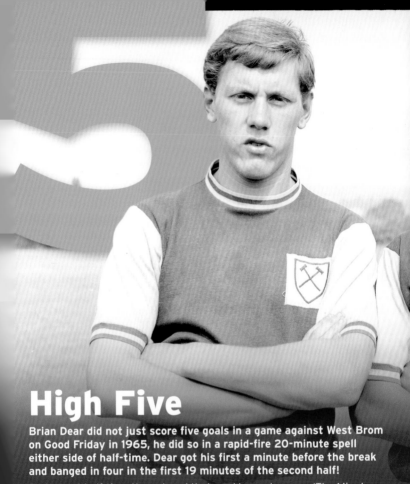

High Five

Brian Dear did not just score five goals in a game against West Brom on Good Friday in 1965, he did so in a rapid-fire 20-minute spell either side of half-time. Dear got his first a minute before the break and banged in four in the first 19 minutes of the second half!

Perhaps at half-time they played that week's number one, 'The Minute You're Gone' by Cliff Richard as the Baggies were certainly gone once Dear got a taste for goals a minute before half-time. Martin Peters got the Irons' other goal with Jeff Astle scoring for the visitors. Astle would score again on Easter Monday as the Throstles turned the tables, winning the return match 4-2.

GEORGE KAY

Centre-Half

For a club renowned for having so many creative players West Ham have probably had more than their fair share of excellent centre-halves during their long history.

The position signified by the number five shirt has witnessed George Kay, Dick Walker, Malcolm Allison, Ken Brown, Tommy Taylor and Alvin Martin being amongst those to play at centre-half with distinction.

5-5

1966 had already been a great year for English football supporters but a week before Christmas in the year England became world champions West Ham and Chelsea served up a five-all draw at Stamford Bridge.

Only a last gasp Bobby Tambling equaliser denied the Irons victory on a day John Sissons made one and scored two, the second from 40 yards! West Ham also drew 5-5 with Newcastle in 1960 and Aston Villa in 1931.

JOHN SISSONS

Amateur Cup Finals

Five FA Amateur Cup finals were staged at West Ham. The Boleyn Ground hosted the FA's prestigious top amateur competition regularly during the 1930s.

Finals were held at the club in 1930, 1932, 1934 and 1937 with a replay of the 1936 final also held at West Ham. Ilford, Casuals and Dulwich Hamlet (three times) lifted the trophy in East London.

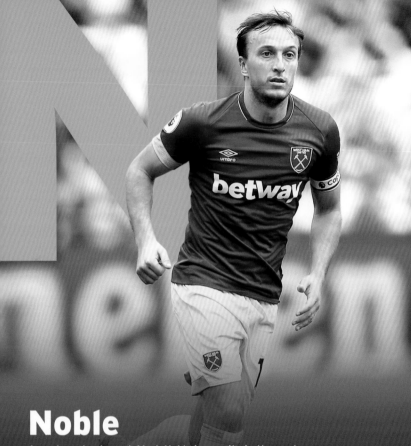

Noble

A modern-day legend, Mark Noble is a rarity in the contemporary game as a one-club man. Born in 1987, Mark has been with the club for his entire career, only having brief loans with Hull and Ipswich when he was a young player making his way in the game.

Deserving of an England cap he is unfortunate to have never added a full cap to the 47 he won at junior levels when he captained his country up to Under 21 level. With over 400 games and more than 50 goals to his credit – many of them penalties – Noble is heading towards the upper reaches of West Ham appearance makers. Twice named Hammer of the Year, in 2016 he received the Freedom of the Borough of Newham for his services to the borough.

Nolan

Forceful goalscoring midfielder Kevin Nolan joined West Ham in June 2011 after a couple of years with Newcastle preceded by a decade with his first club Bolton where he had been a stalwart of Sam Allardyce who brought him to the Irons.

Nolan scored 31 times in 157 games for the club before leaving in August 2015. He went on to be player/manager at both Leyton Orient and Notts County.

Nouble

Much was expected of Frank Nouble when he came to West Ham as a young player in 2009 but in three years he managed just 13 league appearances and went on loan seven times.

In 2018, he was with his 16th different club at Colchester, a tally that included two in China.

Neighbour

Winger Jimmy Neighbour came to West Ham late in his career in the late seventies and early eighties. Having previously topped a century of games with Spurs and Norwich he fell just three short of that tally with the Irons.

Neighbour had played briefly for Seattle Sounders and later served West Ham as Youth Development Officer.

THAMES IRONWORKS 1895

Old Castle Swifts

Old Castle Swifts were a professional club who played in West Ham at a ground called Dunottar Park.

Initially founded in 1892 under the name Castle Swifts the club did not last long, coming to an end after merging with Old St Luke's. As they folded many of their players joined the newly formed Thames Ironworks, the forerunners to West Ham United.

O'Farrell

Later a manager of Manchester United, Leicester; who he took to a cup final, and the Iran national team, Republic of Ireland international Frank O'Farrell was part of that famed group of future managers schooled at the Boleyn Ground in the fifties under Ted Fenton.

A wing-half, O'Farrell played over 200 times for the Irons.

Ogbonna

Italy international centre-back Angelo Ogbonna made his name with Torino where he became captain. Capped at full level by Italy for the first time in 2011 he was transferred to Turin city rivals Juventus two years later for a reported fee of €13m.

In the history of one of Italy's great footballing cities it was the first time a Torino skipper moved to their arch rivals. Twice a Serie A winner with Juve, Ogbonna was an unused sub in the 2015 Champions League final with Barcelona, he was also part of the Italy squad at the 2012 and 2016 European championships.

Olympics

James Tomkins represented West Ham as part of Great Britain's squad at the 2012 Olympics. Having just won promotion in a season where he had been runner-up as Hammer of the Year, Tomkins represented GB twice, once in a warm-up game against Brazil followed by a tournament win over the United Arab Emirates.

The GB team in the competition were managed by former West Ham man Stuart Pearce. Of course a legacy of Great Britain's magnificent staging of the 2012 Games was that West Ham duly moved to the London Stadium with the ambition of adding to the many fantastic moments experienced and enjoyed around the world.

Peters

Had West Germany not equalised in the last minute of the 1966 World Cup final, Martin Peters would forever have been known as the man who scored the winning goal when England became World Champions. Of course extra-time allowed Martin's club-mate Geoff Hurst to go on and become the only man to score a hat-trick in a World Cup final and the third member of West Ham's English World Cup winning contingent – Bobby Moore – to lift the trophy.

A cultured footballer, Peters made his debut for West Ham at Cardiff in April 1962 and went on to play over 700 league matches, over 300 of them for the Irons. He also won the first 33 of his 67 England caps while with West Ham. Famously described by Sir Alf Ramsey as being 'ten years ahead of his time' on more than one occasion Peters was the man of the moment without most people fully appreciating it.

Pellegrini

Manuel Pellegrini became manager of West Ham in May 2018. He was a Premier League winner four years earlier with Manchester City.

Born in 1973 Pellegrini's loyalty as a player was to his one club Universidad de Chile in the capital of Chile, Santiago. He won 28 caps for his country as a centre-back. An outstanding managerial career on both sides of the Atlantic included taking Villarreal to the semi-finals of the Champions League.

Potts

Steve Potts played 505 times for West Ham including one short of 400 in the league.

With the club from 1985 to 2002, Steve saw out his playing days with a season at Dagenham & Redbridge before returning to his first love West Ham to take charge of a variety of the club's younger sides.

Pardew

Alan Pardew managed West Ham between September 2003 and December 2006.

Play-Off runners-up in his first campaign, the Play-Offs were won in 'Pards'' second season before a high point in 2005/06 when a top-half Premier League finish was accompanied by an FA Cup final appearance, lost on penalties to Liverpool.

Paynter

A keen athlete who had competed at the Memorial Grounds where Thames Ironworks played in Victorian times, Charlie Paynter began working for the club as an assistant trainer in those far off days before the beginning of the Boleyn Ground.

It was at the Boleyn Ground that after two decades as trainer Paynter took over as manager from Syd King, Paynter being the club's manager from 1932 to 1950.

Parkes

A record fee for a goalkeeper of £525,000 was lashed out by John Lyall on Phil Parkes in 1979 even though West Ham were a second division (now Championship) club at the time.

Parkes proved to be worth every penny. After 436 appearances Lyall signed him up again, this time for Ipswich in 1990.

Pike

With over 350 appearances between the mid-seventies and mid-eighties, midfielder Geoff Pike gave sterling service to the club, not least in 1980/81 when he was ever-present in the promotion season and runner-up in the Hammer of the Year award.

A year earlier he had helped the Hammers win the FA Cup, while he also played in FA Youth Cup and League Cup finals for West Ham.

Puddefoot

A modern day striker with Syd Puddefoot's West Ham record of 107 goals in 194 league and FA Cup games would be worth millions.

Having started before World War One, Syd was top scorer three years in a row from 1919 to 1922. This led to a record-breaking transfer to big-spending Falkirk where he was close to maintaining a goal for every two games before returning south of the border, initially with Blackburn – with whom he won the FA Cup and was capped by England. He then returned to the Boleyn Ground for a second spell as a veteran before becoming manager of Turkish giants Galatasaray and in England with Northampton.

JACK TRESADERN

Left-Half

Bobby Moore was so good in the old left-half position that his number six shirt has been retired. No longer can anyone stride out in the famous Claret and Blue six shirt immortalised by England's World Cup winning captain.

However, West Ham have had some other great players in this position, a list that includes: Frank O'Farrell, Albert Cadwell, Jack Tresadern and Joe Cockroft.

Synonymous With Six

Just as a Brazil shirt does not seem complete without the number ten of Pele or a Netherlands shirt without Johan Cruyff's number 14, a number six West Ham shirt is forever synonymous with Bobby Moore.

'Mooro' would take his place alongside Pele and Cruyff in an all-time World XI.

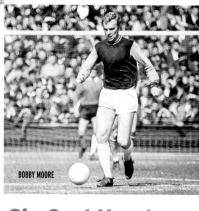
BOBBY MOORE

Six Goal Hurst

Famed worldwide for scoring a hat-trick in the 1966 World Cup final, a simple first division hat-trick for Geoff Hurst would just be another hat-trick - so he scored two in one match.

Hurst stunned Sunderland with six goals as the Wearsiders club record defeat of 8-0 was equalled in 1968.

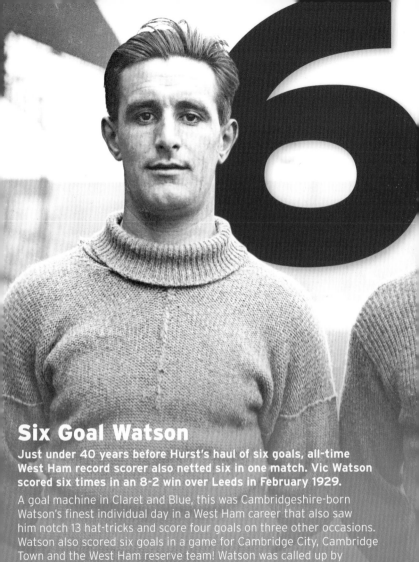

Six Goal Watson

Just under 40 years before Hurst's haul of six goals, all-time West Ham record scorer also netted six in one match. Vic Watson scored six times in an 8-2 win over Leeds in February 1929.

A goal machine in Claret and Blue, this was Cambridgeshire-born Watson's finest individual day in a West Ham career that also saw him notch 13 hat-tricks and score four goals on three other occasions. Watson also scored six goals in a game for Cambridge City, Cambridge Town and the West Ham reserve team! Watson was called up by England six times and scored four goals in the five games he played.

Quashie

Southwark-born Nigel Quashie commanded a £1.5m fee when Alan Curbishley bought him from WBA but a foot injury and further new signings restricted him to a mere eight games for the Irons.

Capped up to B level by England he later switched his allegiance to Scotland and won 14 caps.

Quina

Midfielder Domingos Quina was born in Guinea-Bissau, started his career with Benfica and came to England with Chelsea before coming to West Ham. He has still just 16 when he debuted in the Europa League in July 2016 against NK Domzale of Slovenia.

A European Championship winner at Under 17 and Under 19 level with Portugal, Quina transferred to Watford in the summer of 2018 scoring on his debut against Reading in the Carabao Cup.

Quinn

England B international left-back Wayne Quinn joined West Ham on loan from Newcastle in 2003/04 playing 22 league games before dropping out of the professional game.

The Magpies had paid £800,000 to capture Quinn from his first club Sheffield United but loaned him back to the Blades prior to his loan to the Irons.

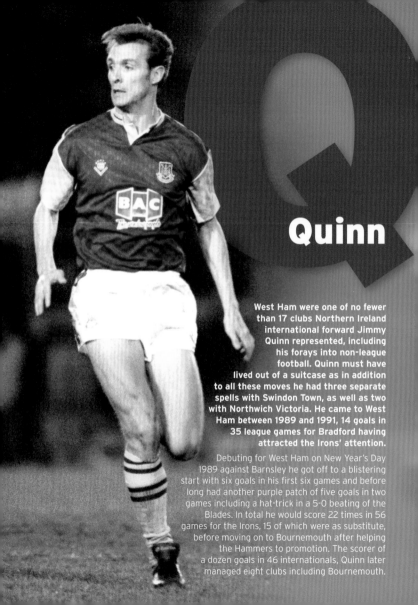

Quinn

West Ham were one of no fewer than 17 clubs Northern Ireland international forward Jimmy Quinn represented, including his forays into non-league football. Quinn must have lived out of a suitcase as in addition to all these moves he had three separate spells with Swindon Town, as well as two with Northwich Victoria. He came to West Ham between 1989 and 1991, 14 goals in 35 league games for Bradford having attracted the Irons' attention.

Debuting for West Ham on New Year's Day 1989 against Barnsley he got off to a blistering start with six goals in his first six games and before long had another purple patch of five goals in two games including a hat-trick in a 5-0 beating of the Blades. In total he would score 22 times in 56 games for the Irons, 15 of which were as substitute, before moving on to Bournemouth after helping the Hammers to promotion. The scorer of a dozen goals in 46 internationals, Quinn later managed eight clubs including Bournemouth.

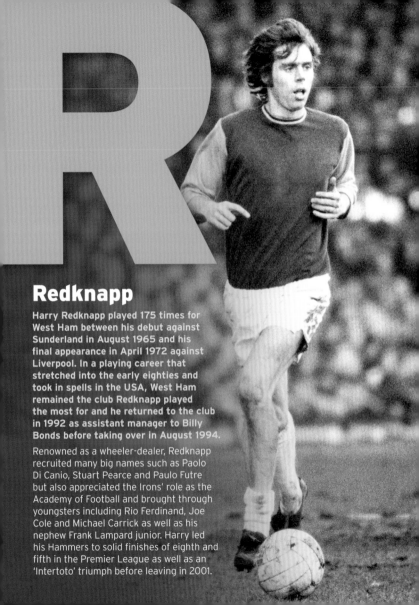

R

Redknapp

Harry Redknapp played 175 times for West Ham between his debut against Sunderland in August 1965 and his final appearance in April 1972 against Liverpool. In a playing career that stretched into the early eighties and took in spells in the USA, West Ham remained the club Redknapp played the most for and he returned to the club in 1992 as assistant manager to Billy Bonds before taking over in August 1994.

Renowned as a wheeler-dealer, Redknapp recruited many big names such as Paolo Di Canio, Stuart Pearce and Paulo Futre but also appreciated the Irons' role as the Academy of Football and brought through youngsters including Rio Ferdinand, Joe Cole and Michael Carrick as well as his nephew Frank Lampard junior. Harry led his Hammers to solid finishes of eighth and fifth in the Premier League as well as an 'Intertoto' triumph before leaving in 2001.

Roeder

Essex-born boyhood West Ham fan Glenn Roeder came to the Boleyn Ground in 1999 as assistant to Harry Redknapp.

Succeeding 'arry in 2001, Roeder led the club to seventh place in the Premier League in his first season in charge but in April 2003 Glenn was diagnosed with a brain tumour. Returning after relegation he took charge again in July and August 2003 before leaving the club.

TEAM OF 1962/63

Replays

West Ham lost the first ten third-round replays they ever played in the FA Cup.

Eventually persistence paid off in 1963 when Fulham were beaten in a replay at Craven Cottage.

Ruffell

Jimmy Ruffell was a star of the years between the World Wars when he made almost 550 games and scored over 160 goals for the club, making many more as a marauding left-winger.

His record of 505 league appearances for the Irons stood from before World War Two until Bobby Moore took over his record in 1973.

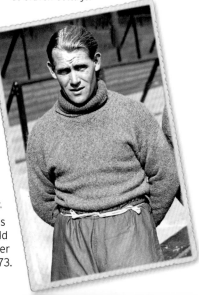

Record

A new club record was set in the summer of 2018 when a reported £36m was invested in Brazil's 2016 Olympic gold medal winner midfielder Felipe Anderson from Lazio.

Anderson started with Pele's old club Santos and helped them win the Copa Libertadores when he was 18.

Rawbau

Rock band Rawbau from Croatia recorded a song called 'Fiery Madness' to commemorate Croatia's appearance at Euro 2008.

Playing a red Gibson Explorer their rhythm guitarist also wrote lyrics and occasionally took over as vocalist. If you have not heard of Rawbau you might have heard of that rhythm guitarist - Slaven Bilic!

Robson

Top scorer in the country in 1973 with 28 goals Bryan 'Pop' Robson bounced between West Ham and his hometown team Sunderland throughout the seventies.

One of the most clinical strikers never to be given an opportunity by England, Robson was a supremely fit, agile and sharp striker who was a model professional. The nickname 'Pop' did not stem from his ability to pop the ball into the back of the net but because as a child he and his two friends had been nicknamed, 'Snap', 'Crackle' and 'Pop' after the slogan of a breakfast cereal.

Retired Shirts

Shirt numbers six and 38 have been retired by West Ham in tribute to two players who remain in the club's thoughts every day: Bobby Moore and Dylan Tombides.

Bobby had the fullest of playing careers, captaining West Ham to some of the greatest moments in their history as well as captaining England on the greatest day of the country who gave football to the world.

While Bobby was synonymous with the number six shirt, Dylan Tombides wore number 38. Hailing from Australia, he was one of those people from around the globe who had fallen in love with the game. A highly promising and much loved young player, Dylan passed away far too young at the age of just 20 in 2014. He had made his debut for West Ham in 2012.

HARRY HOOPER

Outside-Right

Forever associated with playing on the right wing, the number seven shirt has a special magic in football as so often it is wingers that can unlock defences - even if Sir Alf Ramsey's 1966 England World Cup winners were wingless wonders.

Herbert Ashton, Peter Brabrook and fifties star Harry Hooper are amongst those to have thrilled the Chicken Run as they sped down the right flank.

Seven Goal Syd

Syd Puddefoot scored a sensational seven goals in an 11-0 win over Crystal Palace in 1918. The seven-goal haul equalled the record in the London Combination, set by Chelsea's Bob Thompson against Luton two years earlier.

While seven is a notable number in Syd's story so is 17. In 1933/34 while manager of Galatasaray in Turkey he ended up in a brawl in a match against Fenerbahce that saw 17 of the 22 players suspended!

JOHN DICK, 1961

Seven Minutes To Play

There were just seven minutes remaining on 2 January 1954 when West Ham's home match with Stoke City was abandoned with the Irons wining 4-1!

John Dick and Tommy Dixon had scored twice each but those goals were expunged from the records as was the victory. Dick did score once when the match was replayed in April but this time Ted Fenton's team had to settle for a point as the lucky Potters this time drew 2-2.

Magnificent Seven

Not only did West Ham win the FA Cup for the first time in 1964 but they did it with their 'B' team. Seven members of the side had names beginning with the letter B: Ken Brown, John Bond, Jack Burkett, Eddie Bovington, Peter Brabrook, Johnny Byrne and Ronnie Boyce who scored the winning goal.

Just for good measure, around that era West Ham could also call upon: Peter Bennett, Dave Bickles, Jimmy Bloomfield, Martin Britt and Dennis Burnett.

Sanchez

Vastly experienced Colombia midfielder Carlos Sanchez arrived at West Ham in the summer of 2018 from Fiorentina. Known as 'the Rock', Sanchez started in Medellin with the Academy of Alexic Garcia before moving to Uruguay where he played for River Plate Montevideo where Edison Cavani was one of his teammates.

Having broken into the Colombia side Sanchez secured a move to Europe when Valenciennes took him to France in 2007. From there he moved to Spain with Elche before coming to England for the first time with Aston Villa for a reported fee of just under £5m. With Villa struggling, the Colombian was loaned to Fiorentina making the move permanent soon after. Before coming to West Ham the well-travelled player had another taste of life in Spain on loan to Espanyol.

Sissons

18-year-old John Sissons'
goal for West Ham against
Preston in the 1964 FA Cup
final made the winger the
youngest-ever Wembley
FA Cup final scorer.

Having debuted a year almost
to the day before his cup final
heroics, Sissons went on to play
over 260 times for the club,
scoring more than 50 goals.

Sexton

Dave Sexton's influence on the game
went way beyond the 77 games he
played for West Ham in the 1950s.

Another graduate of the array of
future managers and coaches schooled
under Ted Fenton, like Frank O'Farrell
Sexton went on to manage Manchester
United and also worked with the
England team under Bobby Robson.

Stewart

**Penalty king blaster Ray Stewart
managed a magnificent 84 goals
despite mainly playing as a
right-back in his 431 appearances
between 1979 and 1991.**

Capped by Scotland while with
West Ham, Stewart's quality had
persuaded John Lyall to pay
Dundee United a then huge
£430,000 for Ray when he had
barely left his teens behind.

Sullivan

Joint-Chairman of West Ham United, Mr David Sullivan is a long-term supporter of the club.

Having initially invested in the club over two decades earlier Mr Sullivan snapped up the opportunity to gain financial control of the club in 2010 providing much needed impetus after the difficulties of the Icelandic owned period of the club. A patron of Prostate Cancer UK, Mr Sullivan is also a supporter of the Teenage Cancer Trust.

Statue

Jointly commissioned by West Ham United and Newham Council and sculpted by Philip Jackson, the quartet of players in the wonderful 'World Cup Sculpture' features the trio of West ham heroes who won the World Cup with England in 1966:

Captain Bobby Moore and goalscoring heroes Geoff Hurst and Martin Peters along with full-back Ray Wilson, then of Everton.

TEAM OF 1908/09

Southern League

Prior to being admitted to the Football League, West Ham were Southern League members from 1900 to 1915.

The old Thames Ironworks club had won the Southern League and as West Ham, the first match was won 7-0 against Gravesend on 1 September 1900.

Scissor Kick

The BBC's Goal of the Season in 1999/2000 and Sky Sports' Goal of the Decade in a December 2009 vote, Paolo Di Canio's spectacular scissor kick against Wimbledon in March 2000 was a goal which summed up the rare talent of the enigma that is Paolo Di Canio.

As Trevor Sinclair's deep angled cross came to Di Canio at the Boleyn Ground he attempted the sort of shot only a player of his immense self-belief would even dream of. Most players would have looked to bring the ball down and either bring a teammate into play or look to manoeuvre a shooting opportunity but for Di Canio this already was a shooting chance as he took off, seemed to hover in the air and then demonstrating world-class technique caught the ball full on the volley and watched it whistle into the net. What a goal. It was not the Goal of the Decade for nothing!

Sealey

One day someone will equal Alan Sealey's place in the West Ham record books. Until that day Sealey will stay as the only man to score the winner in a European final for the Irons. Sealey scored twice before a full house at Wembley on 19 May 1965 as TSV Munchen were defeated 2-0.

Hampton-born Sealey had played in six of the eight games leading up to the final, also scoring against Sparta Prague. The cup final goals were a great wedding present for Alan who had married a week earlier.

Having joined from Leyton Orient in 1961 Sealey played over 100 league games for the Irons but broke a leg playing cricket and finished his career with Plymouth and later in non-league. Sealey passed away far too early at the age of just 53 in 1996. Goalkeeper Les Sealey who had two brief spells at West Ham but passed away when he was only 43 in 2001, was Alan's nephew.

Sheringham

With over 50 England caps, over 700 league games and only a dozen short of 300 league goals, Teddy Sheringham enjoyed a first class career which included 87 games and 30 goals in competitions for West Ham in the twilight of his career, even still playing as a forward into his forties.

In 2006 at the age of 40 years and 266 days he played for West Ham in the FA Cup final, becoming the oldest player to appear in the show-piece occasion.

Snodgrass

Scotland international Robert Snodgrass cost West Ham a reported fee of over £10m in January 2017.

But by August was surplus to requirements and spent 2017/18 impressing on loan to Aston Villa before returning to West Ham for a fresh start in 2018/19.

Sinclair

A Dulwich-born bundle of energy, Trevor Sinclair had substantial spells with Manchester City, QPR and Blackpool but played more for West Ham than anyone else.

Trevor topped 200 appearances for the club in six seasons ending in 2003.

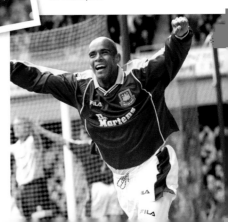

Inside-Right

The number eight shirt equated to the inside-right position for decades. The notion of an inside-forward has largely disappeared from the modern game, as has the description of someone being a wing-half, but this is just fashion.

The midfield area that the players in these old-fashioned positions used to operate is still packed. More often than not modern day teams play with five men in this area of the pitch which is the same as it was before the centre-half started to drop back between the full-backs and you had three half-backs and two inside-forwards. Stan Earle and goal hungry Danny Shea are examples of players who excelled at inside-right.

Devonshire Cream

Alan Devonshire won just eight England caps, an astonishingly low total for a player of such verve and style, one who gave enormous pleasure to the fans who watched him thrill at West Ham.

The son of a former Crystal Palace player, Leslie, Alan started at Selhurst Park as a teenager before making his name with West Ham with whom he won the FA Cup, promotion and was a League Cup runner-up in the early 80s, the era in which he won his eight caps was between May 1980 and November 1983.

TEAM OF 1958

Millers' Tale

Not so famous as the 8-0 top-flight win over Sunderland in 1968 when Geoff Hurst hit a double hat-trick, Rotherham United were also thrashed 8-0 on 8 March 1958, in what is West Ham's record second division victory.

As in the 8-0 v Sunderland there were just three goalscorers: John Dick got four with Vic Keeble and John Smith each claiming braces.

FA Cup Record

A proud FA Cup team, West Ham's record win in the competition was an 8-1 first round victory over Chesterfield on 10 January 1914.

A match in which Syd Puddefoot scored five times.

Team Of The Year

West Ham were named 'Team of the Year' in the BBC Sports Personality awards in 1965 after winning the European Cup Winners' Cup at Wembley.

The Hammers were only the second English team to lift a European trophy and the first to do so on home soil.

Thames Ironworks

Thames Ironworks FC lost their first-ever match in 1895 but won their final one five years later by 5-1. In between they won three trophies including the West ham Charity Cup in 1896.

They were wound up in June 1900 but by 5 July the same year, out of their ashes rose West Ham United! The Thames Ironworks and Shipbuilding Company Limited existed between 1837 and 1912 and in 1860 launched HMS Warrior, the world's first all iron war-ship.

THAMES IRONWORKS 1896 WITH THE WEST HAM CHARITY CUP

Tombides

In April 2014 West Ham lost a promising 20-year-old Australia Under 23 international to cancer. Dylan Tombides was a popular and talented footballer who had a bright future.

He had played at an Under 17 World Cup tournament and after being named as a substitute for a Premier League match a month after his 17th birthday was given his debut in a League Cup tie the following year. Always remembered at West Ham, his shirt number of 38 was retired in his honour.

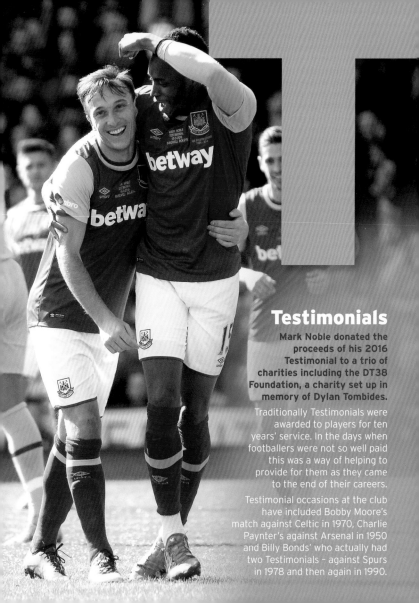

Testimonials

Mark Noble donated the proceeds of his 2016 Testimonial to a trio of charities including the DT38 Foundation, a charity set up in memory of Dylan Tombides.

Traditionally Testimonials were awarded to players for ten years' service. In the days when footballers were not so well paid this was a way of helping to provide for them as they came to the end of their careers.

Testimonial occasions at the club have included Bobby Moore's match against Celtic in 1970, Charlie Paynter's against Arsenal in 1950 and Billy Bonds' who actually had two Testimonials - against Spurs in 1978 and then again in 1990.

Taylor

Tommy Taylor was a seventies stalwart, playing four short of 400 games during the decade for the Irons.

Before and after his time at Upton Park, Tommy played for Leyton Orient who he later returned to manage. He also had a spell on loan with Team Hawaii while with West Ham as well as a stint with Beerschot in Belgium before going into management.

As a manager, as well as working in England, his travels took him to Spain, Finland and Norway. He also took charge of the national team of Grenada.

Ticker

A debutant against Preston in 1960, four years later Ronnie Boyce notched the winning goal in the FA Cup final against the same club.

Nicknamed 'Ticker' due to his work-rate which made the team tick, Boyce also played in the European Cup Winners' Cup final in 1965, making his 342nd and final appearance in 1972. He continued to serve the only club he played for as coach, caretaker manager and chief scout.

Taylor

Alan Taylor came to West Ham from his first league club Rochdale and went on to have an extensive career that included two spells with Vancouver Whitecaps.

In total he played 124 games for the Irons between 1974 and 1979, scoring 36 goals, six of them in the latter stages of the 1975 FA Cup run including both goals in the final against Fulham.

Tevez

In between starting in 2001 at Boca Juniors where he was playing again in 2018, Argentina international Carlos Tevez played in Brazil, Italy and China as well as England where City 'welcomed him to Manchester' after signing him from United.

It had been against United that Carlos scored his most important goal for the Irons, a last day of the season winner that kept the club up in 2007.

UEFA Cup

Now known as the Europa League, this competition grew out of what was formerly called the UEFA Cup. West Ham have competed twice in each version of this competition. 1999/2000 and 2006/07 were the years in which West Ham lined up in the UEFA Cup.

On the first occasion qualification was secured via winning the Intertoto Cup, with West Ham eliminated in the second round. Later in the decade qualification came as FA Cup runners-up but immediate elimination came in a disappointing tie with Palermo from Sicily.

Upton Park

West Ham's former home ground was known throughout the country mainly as Upton Park rather than the Boleyn Ground.

Strictly speaking the Boleyn Ground was in the district of Upton Park.

Upson

Now often seen as a TV pundit, England international defender Matt Upson joined West Ham from Birmingham City on the last day of the 2007 January window for a fee reported to be worth up to £7.5m.

Injured on both his Irons debut and his comeback match, Upson was unable to play a full game until his second season but became captain and played almost 150 games before being transferred to Stoke after West Ham went down in 2011.

USA

Much of the USA's progress in soccer is owed to former West Ham player Phil Woosnam. Having coached the USA team in 1968, a year later he became Commissioner of the North American Soccer League. Establishing TV contracts with major networks, he helped to establish teams in New York, LA, Seattle and over the Canadian border in Canada.

West Ham were one of three clubs the cousin of golfer Ian Woosnam played over 100 league games for, having left his job as a physics teacher to turn professional when becoming a Hammer.

Centre-Forward

The number nine shirt is a prized possession. It indicates you are the fulcrum of the attack. A centre-forward himself, Brian Clough used to say that the purpose of the other players was to get the ball to the number nine.

Vic Watson's 326 goals settles all arguments as to who has been West Ham's best number nine but, Vivian Gibbins, Vic Keeble, Bill Robinson and David Cross are examples of other players who the shirt and the number fitted very nicely.

DAVID CROSS

IAN WRIGHT

Top Scorers

Nine goals is not enough for your top scorer over a season unless the team have an exceptional record of sharing the goals around.

In 2016/17 Michail Antonio became the fourth player to be the Irons top scorer with nine goals. In 1998/99 Ian Wright top scored with nine while two seasons earlier Paul Kitson and Julian Dicks shared top spot with nine goals each.

Penalty Prowess

Penalty shoot-outs are the modern way to settle cup matches that are drawn. One of the most dramatic shoot-outs came against Everton on 13 January 2015.

After a 2-2 draw following extra-time it took goalkeeper Adrian to score the winning penalty as West Ham won 9-8. His Everton counterpart Joel Robles had hit the bar with his spot-kick.

Record Gap

Despite defeat by 3-1 at Bramall Lane, Reg Attwell's debut at Sheffield United on St George's Day, 23 April 1938, did not go too badly. Certainly he would have hoped to make a second appearance sooner than being well into a ninth year since that game when he was next called upon.

However, Attwell's appearance at Plymouth Argyle on the opening day of the first post-WW2 league season on 31 August 1946 ended the longest ever wait between two appearances for a West Ham player. He would only play three more times.

9

MATCH ACTION, 1939

Vegetarian

The founder of West Ham United was also the first President of the London Vegetarian Society where he worked with a young Mahatma Gandi. The founder of the Vegetarian Magazine, Arnold Hills also played in the 1877 FA Cup final for Oxford University and played once for England.

Just for good measure in the late 1870s he held the national records for the mile and three mile distances.

As Managing Director of Thames Ironworks, Hills lived amongst his workforce and in 1895 along with Dave Taylor helped to start up Thames Ironworks Football Club. He helped to finance them until they developed into West Ham United, at which point he stepped back but became a major shareholder when the club became a Limited Company and rented the Memorial Grounds to the club.

In more recent times former Hammer Jermain Defoe announced he had become a Vegan.

Van Der Elst

Francois Van Der Elst became a popular figure at West Ham despite scoring twice against the club in the 1976 European Cup Winners' Cup final for Anderlecht.

Six years later West Ham paid £400,000 to sign him from New York Cosmos and he went on to play in the 1982 World Cup for Belgium while on West Ham's books. He scored 17 goals in 70 games while at the club.

Valencia

Ecuador international Enner Valencia came to West Ham in 2014 for a reported £12m the year after being South America's top scorer.

He packed a powerful shot but did not score enough goals in England and moved on to Mexican club Tigres after a loan with Everton.

Vaz Te

Not everything went well for Ricardo Vaz Te in East London but as the scorer of the winner in the 2012 Play-Off final, the Portugal Under 23 international is assured a place in Hammers folklore.

That winner against Blackpool was Vaz Te's 24th goal of a season that included a hat-trick against Brighton and a goal against Cardiff in the second leg of the Play-Off semi-final.

Inside-Left

Like the number eight worn by the old inside-right, the number ten shirt was the property of an inside-forward, in this case the inside-left. Over the decades though the number ten has taken on a mystique of its own and is now associated with what the Italians call the 'Fantisista' – the player who is the side's main schemer, the prominent creator.

Teams often build their side around this player who is expected to weigh in with a sizeable share of goals. Trevor Brooking is a classic number ten while Len Goulden and Billy Moore also excelled in the position. John Dick and Geoff Hurst are also famous number tens and in their cases were as likely to score as the number nine.

Payne

Joe Payne holds the record for scoring an incredible ten goals in a game. Sadly he did not do this for the Irons although he did play ten league games for West Ham. He did very well in those games however, scoring a very creditable six times.

It was in 1936 that Payne plundered ten goals in 63 sensational minutes against the Pirates of Bristol Rovers while appearing for Luton Town. It was a decade later, on the other side of World War Two, that the former Derbyshire coalminer came to West Ham.

TONY COTTEE

Buried

Bury were already behind when they came to the Boleyn Ground in the League Cup in October 1983, having lost the first leg 2-1 at Gigg Lane.

They saw double figures at West Ham though as Tony Cottee led the way with four goals in a 10-0 win – watched by 10,896.

Ten Goal Wins

Putting ten goals past Bury in the League Cup is not the only time West Ham have scored ten times in a game!

In 1940 Chelsea were walloped 10-3 at Stamford Bridge in a League South fixture. Three years later the same score was achieved in the same competition against Clapton Orient while in 1899 Maidenhead were put to the sword to the tune of 10-0.

MATCH ACTION, 1942

JOHN SISSONS &
GEOFF HURST HOLD
THE FA CUP, 1964

Wembley

Whether it was West Ham being part of the first ever Wembley FA Cup final in 1923, Bobby Moore lifting the same trophy in 1964, becoming the first English team to win a European trophy at the stadium a year later...

...Alan Taylor and Trevor Brooking's cup winning goals in 1975 and 1980 or more recently Mark Noble being part of the 2012 Championship Play-Off success, Wembley stadium holds many magnificent Claret and Blue memories.

War-Time

London Combination Champions in 1917 during World War One, West Ham took advantage of being able to call upon footballers stationed in the area when clubs could take on 'Guest' players to help fulfil fixtures in war-time.

During World War Two, West Ham won the Football League War Cup at Wembley in 1940, beating Blackburn 1-0 in the final.

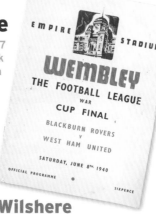

EMPIRE STADIUM

WEMBLEY

THE FOOTBALL LEAGUE

WAR

CUP FINAL

BLACKBURN ROVERS
v
WEST HAM UNITED

SATURDAY, JUNE 8TH 1940

OFFICIAL PROGRAMME   SIXPENCE

Wilshere

England international midfielder Jack Wilshere came to West Ham in 2018 ready to spend what should be the peak years of his career with the Irons after making 125 Premier League appearances for Arsenal.

The PFA Young Player of the Year in 2010/11 he made his England debut when he was only 18 and with 34 caps when he arrived at West Ham at the age of 26 he has time on his side to return to the international side and look to at least double that total of caps.

Webb

George Webb only played 62 games for the Irons but he scored 32 times in those games between 1909 and 1912.

An East-Ender who was the stepson of West Ham director George Hone, Webb went to school under half a mile from the Boleyn Ground and passed away at the age of just 26 in 1915, dying of consumption.

Webb's terrific goals to games ratio was all the more impressive given that while most players claim to be at their best with regular football he never managed to be selected for more than six games in a row.

MATCH ACTION, 1913

Watson

With 326 goals in total for West Ham, 298 of them in the league, Vic Watson holds club records highly unlikely to ever be beaten.

From his debut at Cardiff in 1920 to his final game against Manchester United in 1935 (both goalless draws ironically) Watson was a goal machine who once scored 50 goals in a season (in 1929/30 – from only 44 games) and six goals in a game, against Leeds the season before his half-century haul. An England international, Vic marked the season he scored 50 goals for West Ham by netting twice in a 5-2 victory over Scotland.

Wright

England striker Ian Wright came to West Ham in the twilight of his career, bagging nine of his 236 English league goals with the club where his 22 league appearances helped tilt his career total to just over 500.

Having made his name with Crystal Palace and Arsenal, after his time at the Boleyn Ground he had spells with Celtic and Burnley as well as representing Nottingham Forest on loan from the Hammers.

TED FENTON

Albert Walker

Full-back Albert Walker made 174 appearances for the club during the thirties.

He was still at the club in 1980 after a 28-year stint as part of the back-room staff which commenced in 1952 when manager Ted Fenton brought him back to the club.

Dick Walker

By then centre-half Dick Walker was coming to the end of a first-team career which had started when he was a teammate of Albert, beginning in 1934.

Dick captained the club, made 311 first team appearances, over 100 more during the war and over 200 more at reserve level where he kept playing until 1956/57 after making his final first team appearance against Plymouth in February 1953.

TREVOR BROOKING

X-Factor

Paolo Di Canio, Bobby Moore, Trevor Brooking and Alan Devonshire. These are all examples of players who have brought the X-Factor to West Ham United.

These are players of immense natural talent who simply oozed class and lit up Irons matches with their sheer talent.

X-Rated

STUART PEARCE

Fans everywhere love a good tackle although in modern-day football full-blooded tackles are routinely met with red cards.

Over the years more than one stretcher-bearer may have felt that they were about to be called into action when the likes of Julian Dicks or Stuart Pearce prepared to win possession.

XI

Seeing a line-up marked as a West Ham XI is an indication that the side on show is not a straight-forward West Ham team but an 'XI' made up perhaps of a range of players that can be a mix of young and old and perhaps including guest or former players.

Such teams are most likely to be used in friendly or testimonial matches, for instance when West Ham United played West Ham United All-Stars in March 2016 in a thrilling testimonial match at the Boleyn Ground.

Xande

Xande Silva joined West Ham in the summer of 2018. An Under 20 international with Portugal, he arrived from Vitoria de Guimaraes of the Primeira Liga for whom he had played 26 times in the top flight of Portuguese football. Born in Coimbra, the forward started with Sporting Clube de Portugal and reached the quarter-finals of the European Championships at Under 17 and Under 19 levels in 2014 and 2016 and then the same last eight stage of the World Under 20 Cup. Xande did not take long to announce his arrival on the London stage, netting a six-minute hat-trick against Spurs eleven days after signing to make a real statement on his Under 23 team debut.

Born on 16 March 1997 Silva was 18 when given his first team debut by Guimaraes who threw him into the deep-end in a goalless draw with giants Benfica. His only senior goal came on his sixth appearance, against Rio Ave, in December 2015. 19 of his 26 games in Portugal were as a sub and having come to West Ham as a Development player hopefully he will go on improving and bring the X-Factor to the London Stadium.

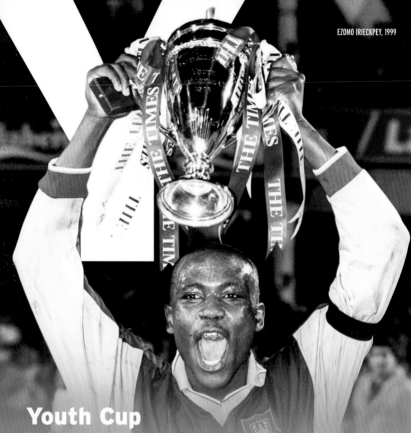

Youth Cup

The FA Youth Cup is a prestigious honour in the domestic club game. West Ham won the trophy in 1999 and 1963 and have also been runners-up in 1996 and 1975. In 1999, Coventry City were blown away in the two-legged final, the Irons winning 9-0 on aggregate after 3-0 and 6-0 victories with a team that included Michael Carrick and Joe Cole.

Harry Redknapp and John Sissons were future stars in the line-up in 1963 when a 3-1 first leg deficit against Liverpool was sensationally overturned with a 5-2 second leg score-line against a Reds side skippered by Tommy Smith. In 1996 the Hammers went down 4-1 on aggregate to Liverpool while in 1975 Ipswich came out on top by 5-1 on aggregate while in the fifties the final was reached in 1957 and 1959 when they were runners-up to Manchester United and Blackburn Rovers.

Young

John Young made 138 appearances for the Hammers between 1919 and 1926.

He scored three goals but two of them came in one game in 1924. Unfortunately for John that brace came in a 3-2 defeat to the dominant team of the era, Huddersfield Town.

TEAM OF 1922/23

Yarmolenko

Ukraine international Andriy Yarmolenko came to West Ham from Borussia Dortmund where he had scored three times in 18 games in his single season in the Bundesliga where he was troubled by injury.

Previously with Dynamo Kiev he had scored 99 goals in 228 league games. Four times Ukrainian Footballer of the Year and three times a Ukrainian Premier League winner, Yarmolenko has an international hat-trick to his name and has big things expected of him after a big-money move.

An exciting winger, happiest on the right but can operate on either flank. A maker as well as a taker of goals, at 6'3" Yarmolenko is big and strong for a wide-man and those assets make him a handful even for the best defenders.

Yews

Winger Tommy Yews scored 51 goals in 361 games for West Ham in a decade beginning in 1923/24.

This was great value for his £150 transfer fee from Hartlepool United even in those days.

GEOFF PIKE

Outside-Left

There are only eleven players in a football team despite the high squad numbers now common. Number eleven used to be the last name on the team sheet but by no means was it the least important.

Like the full-backs, wing-halves and inside-forwards the wingers gave sides symmetry. Malcolm Musgrove, Geoff Pike and John Sissons are all examples of players to shine in the number eleven shirt for the Irons.

Wright Man

Eleven goals made Ken Wright West Ham's top scorer in 1948/49 as the Hammers finished seventh in the second division.

Ken made it a Wright Christmas as he scored twice against Leeds on Christmas Day and did so again against the same opponents two days later.

11-0

Syd Puddefoot put the cry into Crystal Palace as his seven goals were largely responsible for an astonishing 11-0 win over Palace in the Football Combination on 6 April 1918. Not surprisingly it was a record win by any team in the competition.

It took just three minutes for Syd to start scoring. Four-nil up at the break, the Hammers scored even earlier in the second half than they had in the first. So goal happy were they that the eighth goal of the afternoon was the club's 100th of the season. Even after the home side had Jack Macksey sent off at 9-0 the visitors were so demoralised the ten men still added another two goals.

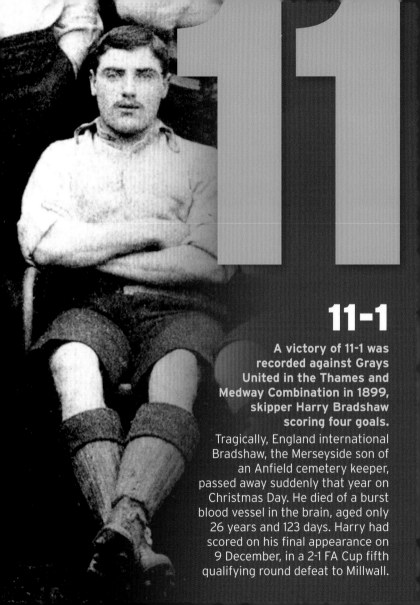

11-1

A victory of 11-1 was recorded against Grays United in the Thames and Medway Combination in 1899, skipper Harry Bradshaw scoring four goals.

Tragically, England international Bradshaw, the Merseyside son of an Anfield cemetery keeper, passed away suddenly that year on Christmas Day. He died of a burst blood vessel in the brain, aged only 26 years and 123 days. Harry had scored on his final appearance on 9 December, in a 2-1 FA Cup fifth qualifying round defeat to Millwall.

Zabaleta

Pablo Zabaleta has played over 50 times for Argentina, including in the 2014 World Cup final.

Zabaleta came to the Irons after almost a decade with Manchester City having established himself in Europe with three years with Espanyol after starting in his home country with San Lorenzo.

Zamora

145 goals in 475 league games included 30 in 130 appearances for the Hammers for Barking-born Bobby. He grew up supporting the Irons for whom he played more games than any of his other clubs.

The West Ham highlights for Zamora came outside those statistics, with four goals in the 2005 Play-Offs including the winner in the final against Preston.

Zaragoza

When West Ham won the European Cup Winners' Cup in 1965, Real Zaragoza were the opposition in the semi-final.

One of the great European nights at the Boleyn Ground saw the Irons take a narrow 2-1 lead to Spain for the second leg where a determined performance earned a 1-1 draw to propel them to one of the finest nights in the club's history at Wembley where the trophy was lifted.

Zola

A fine footballer who scored ten goals in 35 internationals for Italy, Zola was as notable a sportsman as he was a skilful player. It was West Ham where he commenced his managerial career in 2008, replacing Alan Curbishley at the Boleyn Ground.

In keeping with his style as a player Gianfranco looked to bring flair to the club and also showed a willingness to give opportunities to young players. Unfortunately results were not as good as the club or Zola himself would have preferred and his time in the hot-seat came to a close a couple of days after the 2009/10 campaign closed. West Ham won 23 and lost 36 of his 80 games in charge.

Forever
Blowing Bubbles